Sew Chinelo

Chinelo Bally

How to transform your wardrobe with sustainable style

Sew Chinelo

COLLINS & BROWN

First published in the United Kingdom in 2021 by
Collins & Brown
43 Great Ormond Street
London
WC1N 3HZ

An imprint of Pavilion Books Company Ltd

Distributed in the United States and Canada by
Sterling Publishing Co., Inc. 1166 Avenue of the Americas, New York, NY 10036

ISBN 978-1-91116-389-3

A CIP catalogue record for this book is available from the British Library.
10 9 8 7 6 5 4 3 2 1

Reproduction by Rival Colour Ltd, UK
Printed and bound by L.E.G.O. S.p.A, Italy
www.pavilionbooks.com

Photographer: Claire Pepper
Stylist: Alex Fullerton
Illustrations: Kuo Chen
Publisher: Helen Lewis
Design manager: Laura Russell
Production manager: Phil Brown

Hi, I'm Chinelo Bally: a designer/dressmaker, sewing instructor, television craft contributor and author. I began my sewing journey in January 2011, when I bought my first second-hand sewing machine. What actually inspired the venture was my inability to buy clothes that really suited my style and fitted well. I'm a tall, curvy girl, and finding clothes that fitted my physique beyond 'blah' was very difficult before most stores included a range for tall women. This was a blessing in disguise, I guess, because it meant that I had to learn to make my own clothes. Not long after starting my dressmaking journey, I was selected to participate in a BBC Two television show, *The Great British Sewing Bee* season 2, where I came second – and it all took off from there. Needless to say, my little hobby has taken me on an amazing adventure that I am extremely grateful for.

Before I started sewing I would buy an item of clothing because I liked certain aspects of it, then cut it up and have my tailor reattach it to something else. The deconstruction of existing garments for this purpose actually helped me to understand the construction of clothes, and how and why things work. When faced with a garment for repurposing, I see the item as a piece of fabric and always ask myself two things: what can I do with this much fabric, and can I add anything to complement it?

The idea of giving something old a new lease of life or a new purpose is quite exhilarating. We live in an age of fast, disposable fashion, which reflects many aspects of society. At the risk of sounding political or like a crusader, I wish we were less wasteful. Upcycling is a fantastic way to put the brakes on disposable culture and make everyday items more sustainable. Aside from the love of sharing my craft, this was a major catalyst in doing this book. I want to inspire people to go shopping – but within their own wardrobes, in those of willing family and friends, and in the many fantastic charity shops. I want people to take another look at an old dress or an abandoned shirt and reimagine it into something amazing; a truly one-off piece.

This book contains a number of projects that celebrate the craft of upcycling, as it is the way I unknowingly ventured into dressmaking, it gave me a soft landing, and it made me very aware of my creative process. If you're a sewing newbie, why not try the upcycling projects and then progress to the other projects? It's a great way to really master the freehand technique.

Since writing my first book, *Freehand Fashion*, my husband and I have had an amazing little girl who has turned us into big piles of mush. So guess what, guys – I now make children's clothes too! There are a few in here modelled by my beautiful Demi.

I hope you enjoy trying out the projects, and your feedback and pictures are always so helpful. Please post your creations and hashtag #freehandfashion #freehandrefashion #sewchinelo #chinelobally. I'm brimming with excitement as I wait to see all your creations!

Chinelo

About freehand cutting

Freehand cutting is all about marking your measurements directly onto fabric, using simple tools, and developing an understanding of how clothes come together and sit on the contours of the body. It allows you to tailor clothes precisely to your own shape and size – no more fiddling around, adjusting commercial patterns to fit!

Although the idea of freehand garment construction intrigues many in the West, this method has been used traditionally and is still used in many of the less developed parts of the world. Fashion varies greatly around the globe and there is a vast array of traditional dress codes. In Africa and Asia many garments are created, if not entirely freehand, with at least some reference to this approach.

I am most familiar with the Nigerian freehand method, and although this has coloured my own sewing technique and style aesthetically, I have further developed what I learned to achieve a high-quality and very precise individual fit, with an exceptional standard of finishing both on the inside and outside of the garments.

My book covers key techniques and the drafting, cutting and construction of a sleeve block. It contains a plethora of exciting projects that range from easy to more challenging. For me, sewing isn't just about craftsmanship, it's also about design; the silhouettes of the garments we will make are timeless, beautiful shapes that have lasted throughout the history of fashion. We will make beautifully fitted gowns for ultra-glamorous events like a posh party or a prom, flattering tops that ooze femininity, and many more garments that will give your wardrobe a facelift.

Sewing essentials

N owadays sewing is becoming very hi-tech and gimmicky, but I believe that these new-fangled tools are just candy-coated basics. Before I discovered fancy machine feet, I always did my invisible zips with a standard foot. At one of my workshops recently there was a bit of a panic amongst the students because we only had one concealed zipper foot. I soon calmed them down by inserting the invisible zip with the standard foot. They were dead impressed and I've added a new party trick to my list!

I digress; the point is that although modern equipment makes life easier, it isn't essential. You don't have to be put off doing a buttonhole because you don't have a buttonhole foot; you can carefully use the zigzag stitch on your machine or do it by hand. You don't even need a seam ripper for unpicking your mistakes; just slide a razor blade carefully between the layers and the job is done far quicker.

Basic sewing project equipment

Sewing machine
Scissors: large fabric shears and small, sharp scissors
Needles
Pins

Tape measure
Seam ripper
Chalk, pencil or fabric marker (or something to mark with)
Ruler
Iron and ironing board

Also useful

Pinking shears
Overlocker
Zip foot for sewing machine

Techniques

I truly believe that, once you've mastered threading your machine and sewing in a reasonably straight line, you can tackle pretty much any sewing project you want! There are a few basic things like neatening seams and understitching that will help to give your work a professional-looking edge, as well as a couple of other techniques that I would urge you to get to grips with. Here are my top techniques for successful stitching!

Seams

The majority of seams in this book are very simple – just place the pieces to be joined right sides together and sew, taking the seam allowance specified in the project instructions. There is one slightly more specialised seam that's well worth mastering, and that's a French seam. It's commonly found in shirts, and is particularly useful for sheer or lightweight white fabrics, where you don't want the seam allowance to show through when you're wearing the garment, and for lightweight fabrics that fray easily, as all the raw edges of the seam allowances are enclosed.

French seam

01 Place the pieces wrong sides together and sew, taking a 6-mm (¼-in) seam allowance. Press the seam open and trim the seam allowance to 3mm (⅛ in) from the stitching.

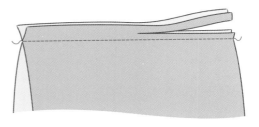

02 Fold the fabric right sides together along the line of stitching that you've just worked. Pin and stitch a second line of stitching, taking a 1-cm (⅜-in) seam allowance.

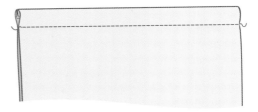

03 Press the seam to one side.

Seam finishes

There are several ways to finish seams in a garment. These are just some of them, but I am highlighting them because I use them a lot. Overlocking is a great way to prevent seams from fraying, and you can buy a dedicated machine to do it. However, an overlocker is quite an investment, especially if you are new to sewing. The good news is that you can use the zigzag stitch on your sewing machine to perform a very similar function. The main difference is that a sewing machine won't trim the seam as well as finishing the edges.

Overlocking

Overlockers are scary machines to those who aren't familiar with them, but once you get the hang of it you won't ever want to be without one. They oversew the edges of the seam with looped stitches to prevent the fabric from fraying; at the same time, two blades trim the seam allowance to reduce the bulk. Overlocking your seams gives them a shop-bought finish on the inside and keeps you safe from those random stray threads from raw seams. Before overlocking, test the tension with a scrap piece of the same fabric; this is important because you don't want to make any mistakes on the actual garment as the overlocker stitching is less forgiving than the sewing machine's.

You can also use your overlocker to create a rolled hem. Each machine will come with instructions for this. If you stretch the fabric as you feed it through you will end up with a beautifully wavy hem, which can add some drama to your garment.

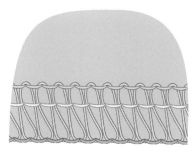

Zig-zagging

Ziz-zagging your seams is an alternative to overlocking. Like overlocking, this stops the seam fraying, but you will not get the shop-bought finish. The trick to zig-zagging your seams is to make sure that the stitch width is good for the fabric you are using. Set the machine to a zigzag stitch and attach a zigzag foot. Line up the foot near the edge of the seam so the zigzag will cover the seam edges when the needle drops. Sew. Test the settings with scraps of the same fabric, and when you are happy with the results trim down your seam allowances to 1.2cm (½ in) and ziz-zag them.

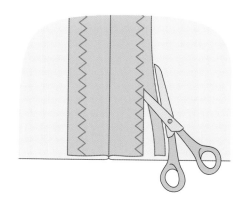

Unpicking and achieving a neat edge on seams

Unpicking

I use a razor blade to unpick most seams, as I find it faster and less damaging to the seam. Use a seam ripper to unpick a couple of stitches, then pull both seams apart gently to expose the thread. Using the razor blade, cut the threads as you work down the seam. If you're more comfortable using a seam ripper throughout, that's fine.

Clipping seams

It's important to clip curved seams because failure to do so will result in a puckered neckline or seam line. Clipping gives a seam flexibility, and it is also used to reduce bulk.

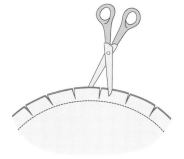

To clip a concave curve, cut small wedges out of the seam that nearly reach the stitch line, being careful not to snip into your stitch line. Clip at regular 2.5–4-cm (1–1½-in) intervals.

To clip a convex curve, simply snip a straight notch into the seam allowance. The notch should just about meet the stitches. This should also be done at regular intervals.

To clip corners, simply cut the seam allowance across the tip of the corner at an angle. Essentially you're trying to get as close to the point as possible without compromising the stitch in the corner.

Understitching

This technique is used to keep the linings and facings from peeking out when the garment is worn; it's particularly important around armholes and necklines. I really do swear by understitching – extreme, I know, but it is so important to understitch any faced edges. I always understitch the seam from the right side of the garment, as I find it easier to keep my row of stitching straight this way, but experiment and see what works best for you.

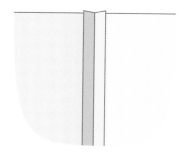

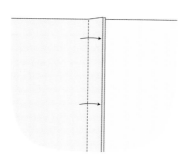

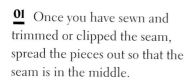

01 Once you have sewn and trimmed or clipped the seam, spread the pieces out so that the seam is in the middle.

02 With your fingers, press the seam allowance towards the lining or facing. Turn the piece over so the right side is facing you.

03 Sew a line of stitching through the lining or facing and both layers of the seam allowance, no more than 3mm ($^1/_8$ in) from the original seam. Fold the fabric back along the original seam line so that it's right side up, and press. The lining or facing will now sit slightly rolled behind the front of the garment. Press this in place; you should now have a clean, finished edge.

Using bias binding as a facing

This is one of my favourite ways of using bias binding. You can either do this on the wrong side of the fabric so that the bias binding is invisible, or on the right side as a design detail. The great thing with doing this is that you can also blind stitch by hand to give you the cleanness of a bagged-out seam, something I love so much. If you have problems hemming curved seams with perfectly straight stitching, then this will be a great help for you.

My ultimate rule for bias binding is DO NOT PIN; pinning makes it difficult to control as you sew, let your hands do what the pins are supposed to do. For best results, use 1.2-cm (½-in) bias binding – but never wider than 2cm (¾ in), unless you are binding a straight edge.

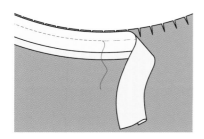

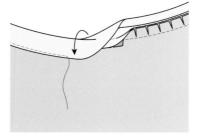

01 Unfold one side of the bias binding. Right sides together, lay the bias binding on the seam, aligning the raw edges.

02 Working in short sections, keeping the edges aligned as you go, begin sewing along the crease line in the binding. Once the binding is sewn on, clip the seams at regular intervals.

03 Press the binding over to the wrong side of the garment, along the stitching line.

04 Working from the wrong side, sew along the edge of the bias binding to hold it down in place. Alternatively you could blind stitch the bias binding in place by hand.

Using bias binding to finish an armhole or neckline

These instructions are for bias binding that is 1.2–2.5cm (½–1 in). Open out one folded edge of the bias binding. Place this with the right side of the binding against the right side of the garment, making sure the raw edges are aligned. Sew along the ditch of the fold.

Fold the bias binding along the stitching line, turning the binding to the wrong side of the fabric.

Press.

On the inside of the garment, hand-sew the bias binding along the folded edge, catching it down so it does not show through on the outside of the garment. Alternatively, machine-stitch 3mm (⅛ in) from the folded edge; this will give you a neat finish on the inside and outside of the garment.

Machine-rolled hem

This is my all-time favourite hem. Since learning this style of hem I have hardly used any other sort; I just love the delicate finish it gives to silks, satins, chiffons and cotton. This method of hemming will not work for any thick fabric and you will really need to sew on the edge very neatly, so get a scrap piece of fabric and practise until you are happy with your stitches.

01 Set your stitch length to 1.5 or 2 (you will need a very tight stitch length for this first row of sewing).

02 Turn under a 1.2-cm (½-in) hem to the wrong side, sewing 3mm (⅛ in) from the fold as you turn. Work slowly and keep the hem depth consistent.

03 Using small, very sharp scissors, cut off the excess fabric as close to the stich line as possible, without cutting into the stitches.

04 Set your stitch length to 2.5 or 3. Turn the hem along the first line of stitching and sew a second line of stitching along the edge, as close as possible to the first line of stitching.

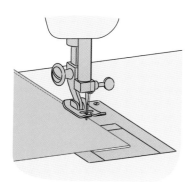

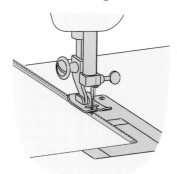

Inserting an invisible zip

There's an abundance of methods when it comes to sewing an invisible zip. I scoured the Internet trying to find one I could understand, because I just couldn't get my head around it. What I learned while sampling other people's instructions was that my aunty was right about not using pins. In fact, when it comes to zips, pins do the exact opposite of what you are using them for. I have taught this method to everyone who has attended my workshops and the general consensus is that it's a lot easier. This is definitely one to throw into your bag of tricks. I always buy the longest length of zip because its easy to shorten and the zip can get to the desired depth. For instance, I prefer my zip to get to my hip line because I like to step into my clothes rather than over the head, and only the longest zip length (usually 60cm/24 in) will give me that.

01 Following the instructions in your project, stitch the seamed section of the garment below the zip by sewing along your zip-allowance fold from 2.5cm (1 in) below the point at which you want your zip to stop.

02 With tailor's chalk, mark your zip stop point (2.5 cm/1 in above the seam you have just sewn) on the right sides of the left and right garment pieces. This is the point at which you stop sewing your zip to the garment, no matter how long your zip is.

03 Lay your garment down right side up and open up the zip allowance folds. Position your zip over the garment right side down. Undo the zip.

04 Take the left side of the zip in your left hand, and the right side in your right hand. The piece in your right hand will be sewn to the left garment piece and vice versa.

Sewing the zip

05 Attach an invisible zipper foot to your machine.

06 There is always a tiny plastic stop at the top end of an invisible zip; line this up with the top edge of the zip-allowance seam. Position the coils of the zip over the zip-allowance fold, then make sure that the groove in the zipper foot sits directly over the zip coils.

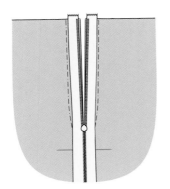

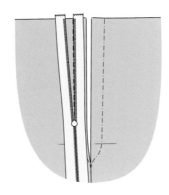

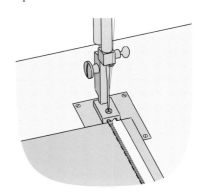

07 Sew your zip in place, making sure that the groove on the foot remains lined up with the zip allowance fold. Be patient with this: it's not a race, so take your time and do it in sections rather than trying to sew the whole zip in one go. I always do a 5-cm (2-in) section, then I stop, check that I'm lined up, and then carry on. It might sound a little long winded, but it's only a few seconds in practise, and well worth it for saving a few minutes of unpicking. Stop sewing when you get to the zip stop mark. Lock your stitch.

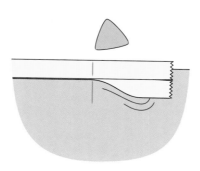

08 Do up the zip. Now using the garment attached to the zip, mark the waist seam (if there is one) and the zip stop point on the back of the side of the zip that hasn't been sewn.

09 Undo the zip again Match up the zip stop mark on the zip with the zip stop mark on the garment. Pin the second side of the zip in place at this point only. Start sewing the zip from this point, making sure the waist seams/marks on both zip and garment match up.

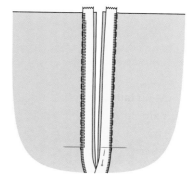

10 When you get to the top, lock the stitch. Do up the zip to make sure both sides are perfectly matched up.

11 Hand tack the 2.5-cm (1-in) opening at the base of the zip, then machine sew over the tacking stitches using a standard zipper foot. Turn the garment over, and press the zip allowance folds back; the zip will be almost invisible from the right side.

Note

I always buy the longest length of invisible zip because you can always cut away the excess when you have finished inserting it. I strongly recommend you get an invisible zipper foot if you're working with a domestic machine.

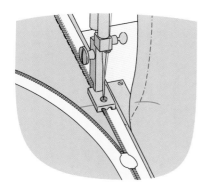

Inserting a lapped zip

With this kind of zip, one side of the zip opening is lapped over the other, concealing the zip teeth. It can be used for the left side of garments such as skirts or for a centre-back opening.

01 Leave an opening in the seam the length of the zip plus 2cm (¾ in). Press the seam open, then press the zip allowances to the wrong side.

02 Open out the right-hand zip allowance. Place the zip right side down on top, with the teeth running centrally down the seam line. Tack it in place if you wish. Fit a standard zipper foot to your machine, to the right of the needle. Stitch the right-hand size of the zip tape in place, about 6mm (¼ in) from the teeth.

03 Fold the zip allowance back and turn the zip right side up. Position the zipper foot to the left of the needle and stitch along the edge of the fold.

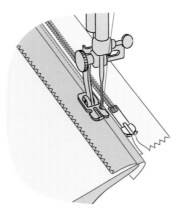

04 Turn the garment wrong side up. Pin and tack the left-hand side of the zip in place.

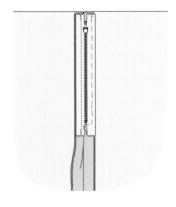

05 Working from the right side, with the zipper foot to the right of the needle, stitch the zip in place. Start by stitching across the base of the zip, pivoting at the bottom, then stitch up to the top of the zip.

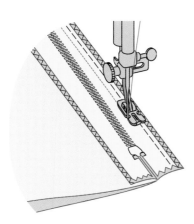

Note
You are only stitching the zip to the zip allowance – not to the garment.

Taking measurements

If you want to use the freehand method, it is important to learn how to take detailed and accurate measurements of yourself. This is the only way you can guarantee that your finished garment will fit you. (A further point to bear in mind is that you may not always have someone handy to take the measurements for you, especially if, like me, you are a bit last-minute.com, always making your clothes on the day you actually need them!) At my workshops I encourage participants to learn how to take their own measurements, but this means making a conscious effort not to distort the body as you do so. If you find it too difficult, then ask someone to help you – and there are some measurements that will definitely require an extra pair of helping hands. I have broken my measuring system in to three groups. There are diagrams to help you on pages 22–23.

Note
Many people wear control underwear under their garments, especially if it's a special occasion. If you will be doing so, it is best to wear it when taking your measurements, because this will affect your proportions and will compromise the fit if not taken into account.

Horizontal
These are the measurements that run horizontally across the body. These are the ones that get divided into 2 or 4 in all of the projects.

Vertical
These measurements run vertically along the body. They are used as reference points, along which you will mark the corresponding divided horizontal measurement.

Other
These are extra measurements that are covered within the projects.

Horizontal measurements

1. Back
from the top corner of one shoulder, straight across to the top corner of the other shoulder

2. Across Back
straight across 2.5cm (1 in) above the armpit crease in the back

3. Across Front
straight across 2.5cm (1 in) above the armpit crease in the front

4. Bust
around the body at the fullest part of the bust

5. Overbust
around the body at the top of the bust

6. Underbust
around the body at the base of the bust

7. Waist
this refers to the natural waist; a good way to find this is to bend your body to the side – the deepest part of the bend is your natural waist

8. Hip
around the biggest section above the thigh

Tip
Always take your measurements standing up, with your posture straight.

Vertical measurements

9. Shoulder to Across Back
from shoulder to 2.5cm (1 in) above the back armpit curve

10. Shoulder to Across Front
from the shoulder to 2.5cm (1 in) above the front armpit curve

11. Shoulder to Overbust
shoulder to the point beginning of the bust

12. Shoulder to Bust
shoulder to the highest point of the bust

13. Shoulder to Underbust
shoulder to the base of the bust, following the contour of the bust

14. Shoulder to Waist
shoulder to the natural waist, following the contour of the bust, underbust and down to the waist

15. Shoulder to Hip
shoulder to hip, following all the contours of the body

16. Shoulder to Knee
shoulder to knee, following all the contours of the body

17. Shoulder to Floor
shoulder to the base of the feet

18. Underarm Length
base of armpit to desired sleeve length

Other measurements

19. Apex
across nipple to nipple

20. Round Sleeve (RS)
around the fullest part at the top of the arm. If you are NOT using stretchy fabric, do not wrap the tape tight because you will need room to manoeuvre

21. Round Elbow (RE)
as above, but around the elbow

22. Sleeve Length (SL)
from the top of the shoulder corner to the desired length of the sleeve

23. Elbow Length (EL)
from the top of the shoulder corner to the elbow

24. Back Length
from the nape to the deepest part of the back hollow

25. Hollow to Dip
from hollow at base of the neck to desired lowest point of sweetheart neckline

Trouser measurements

Back Waist to Seat
while seated on a hard chair, measure from the natural waistline, at the back, to the chair. Usually known as body rise; and measured at side from waist to chair. This is the depth of the crotch.

Inside Leg
crotch to hem along the inside of the leg

Outside Leg
from the waist to the hem along the outside of the leg

Thigh
measure around the fullest part of the upper leg

Note
When taking measurements from the shoulder down, imagine that you are looking down on yourself from a bird's eye view, and place the head of the tape measure in the very centre of your shoulder.

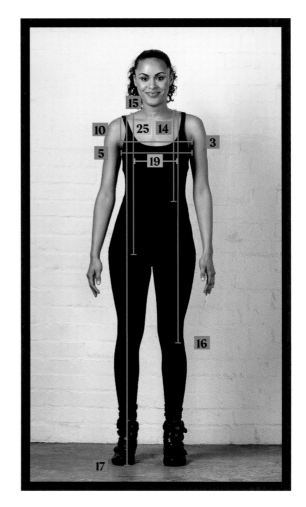

My measurements

Fill in your measurements on this chart, so that you've always got them to hand.

Horizontal measurements

1 Back

2 Across Back

3 Across Front

4 Bust

5 Overbust

6 Underbust

7 Waist

8 Hip

Vertical measurements

9   Shoulder to Across Back
10   Shoulder to Across Front
11   Shoulder to Overbust
12   Shoulder to Bust
13   Shoulder to Underbust
14   Shoulder to Waist
15   Shoulder to Hip
16   Shoulder to Knee
17   Shoulder to Floor
18   Underarm Length

Other measurements

19   Apex
20   Round Sleeve (RS)
21   Round Elbow (RE)
22   Sleeve Length (SL)
23   Elbow Length (EL)
24   Back Length
25   Hollow to Dip

Sleeve Block

Measurements needed

Horizontal measurements (see page 22)
- Round Sleeve
- Round Elbow
- Round Wrist

Vertical measurements (see page 23)
- Sleeve Length
- Underarm Length
- Elbow Length

Amount of fabric needed
- Width = Round Sleeve × 2 + 5cm (2 in)
- Length = Sleeve Length + 4cm (1½ in)

Equipment needed
- Tape measure
- Fabric marker
- Iron and ironing board
- Metre rule
- Scissors

Notes
Always fold fabric right sides together unless otherwise stated. It is important to press every fold to create definite creases.

SLEEVE HEAD

CENTRE LINE

HEM

SLEEVE CAP HEIGHT +

ELBOW LENGTH +

WRIST

Method

01 Fold the fabric in half along the width and then in half along the width again. The top edge is the sleeve head, the bottom edge is the hem, and the side with the second fold is the centre line of the sleeve.

02 Subtract your Underarm Length from your Sleeve Length; the result is your sleeve cap height. Place the head of the tape measure on the sleeve head edge and use the fabric marker to mark your sleeve cap height and elbow length.

03 Visualise these marked vertical measurements as straight lines running horizontally across the fabric; each line has a corresponding horizontal measurement that is measured along it from the centre line edge. Divide your Round Sleeve measurement by two and add 1.2cm (½ in), and mark that measurement with a cross on the sleeve cap height line. Divide your Round Elbow measurement by two and add 1.2cm (½ in), and mark that measurement with a cross on the Elbow Length line. At the hem, measure 11.5cm (4½ in) from the fold and mark.

04 Using the rule, join the crosses with a straight line. From the top of the centre line edge, measure and mark 2.5cm (1 in) along the sleeve head edge.

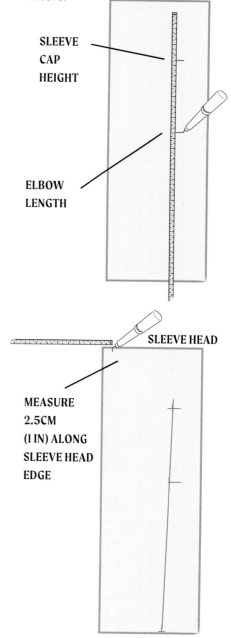

SLEEVE HEAD

SLEEVE CAP HEIGHT

ELBOW LENGTH

SLEEVE HEAD

MEASURE 2.5CM (1 IN) ALONG SLEEVE HEAD EDGE

05 This is the part of the sleeve that requires practice to get the curves right. From the cross on the sleeve cap line, draw a concave slope up to about one-third of the way towards the sleeve head.

SLEEVE HEAD

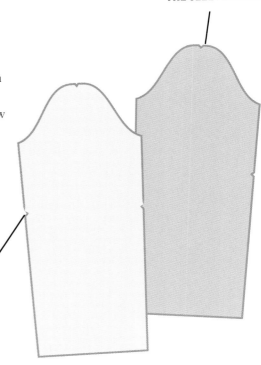

SLEEVE CAP HEIGHT

HEM

ROUND OFF THE LINE AT THE SLEEVE HEAD EDGE

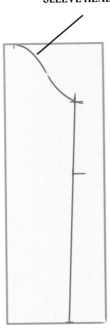

06 Continue the curve upwards as shown, rounding off into the mark on the sleeve head edge.

MAKE A NOTCH AT THE CENTRE OF THE SLEEVE HEAD

07 Cut along the drawn lines through all layers to cut out two sleeves. Notch the centre lines at the sleeve head, and the elbow length on the side seams.

MAKE A NOTCH AT THE ELBOW

Setting in the sleeves

For all sleeves, I always find it easiest to have the sleeve right side out and the garment wrong side out. I then insert the sleeve into the garment armhole so that the right side of the sleeve is facing the right side of the garment, but I am working from the wrong side of both.

01 Sew two rows of long-length stitches (gathering stitch) along the sleeve head, close together and 6 mm (¼ in) and 1cm (³/₈ in) from the edge. Start and end each row 4cm (1½ in) from the sleeve side seam, and leave a tail of thread at the beginning and end of each row.

02 Pull gently on the tails to very slightly gather the sleeve head.

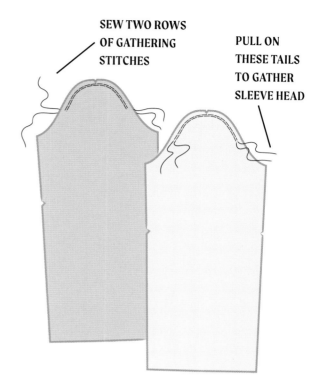

SEW TWO ROWS OF GATHERING STITCHES

PULL ON THESE TAILS TO GATHER SLEEVE HEAD

THE NOTCH IN THE CENTRE OF THE SLEEVE HEAD SHOULD LINE UP WITH THE SHOULDER SEAM

THE SIDE SEAM OF THE SLEEVE SHOULD MATCH UP WITH THE SIDE SEAM OF THE GARMENT

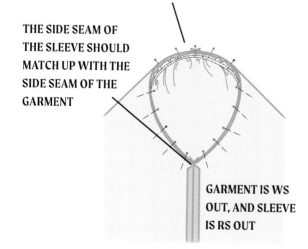

GARMENT IS WS OUT, AND SLEEVE IS RS OUT

03 Sew the side and shoulder seams of the garment, taking a 1.2-cm (½-in) seam allowance. Sew the sleeve underarm seams, neaten the seam allowances and press the seams open. Turn the sleeves right side out.

04 Right sides together, slip the sleeve into the bodice. Match up the side seam of the sleeve with the side seam of the bodice and pin the layers together. Pin the centre line notch in the sleeve to the shoulder seam of the bodice. Ease the sleeve head to fit into the armhole by adjusting the gathering stitches, making sure the fullness is equally spread across the sleeve head and pin in place all the way around.

05 Starting from the side seam, sew the sleeve in place. Alternatively you can tack the sleeve in place and then machine sew it, removing the tacking stitches afterwards.

The Projects

Signature collared top

I have a confession to make: this signature collared top actually resulted from a happy accident that happened years ago whilst attempting a high-necked top. Happy accidents have been key to learning new cuts during my sewing journey. I have made a few tweaks to the design over the years and the result is a beautifully structured abstract collar that could adorn the neckline of any top.

For this project, I am using pure cotton shirting fabric, because it will lend itself well to the desired aesthetics of the design.

Measurements
(see pages 19–23)

Horizontal
Back
Bust
Underbust
Waist
Hips

Vertical
Shoulder to Bust
Shoulder to Underbust
Shoulder to Waist
Shoulder to Hem

Other
Apex

Pattern pieces for signature-collared top
Bodice:
(Widest horizontal body measurement plus 40.5cm/ 16 in) × (Shoulder to hem + 4cm/ 1½ in)
Collar formula:
(Entire neckline circumference plus 40.5cm/16 in) = NC
Collar fabric:
(NC divided by two) × 18cm (7 in)

Materials
Approx. 2.75m (3 yd) pure cotton shirting fabric
Soft interfacing
Lining
Matching thread
Invisible zip: Use the longest length as you can always cut it down to size

Equipment
Basic sewing project equipment

Method

Bodice front and back

Prepare the fabric piece that will be used for the bodice front and back.

Fold the fabric in half with right sides together, so the fold line runs down the length. Press. The fold will be the centre front of the bodice.

On the open end opposite the centre-front fold, fold over both edges by 2.5cm (1 in) and press towards the first fold. This is a zip fold at centre back. The top edge forms the shoulder seam and the bottom edge the hem.

Bring the centre front fold over to line up with the centre back fold, so you now have four layers of fabric. (01)

01

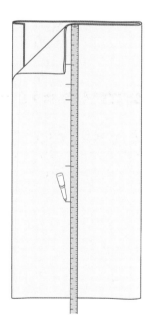

02

Place the vertical measurements

Place the head of the tape measure at the shoulder seam, and measure downwards to mark the vertical measurements. Place a mark at 18cm (7 in), which will serve as the bustline. Mark all the other vertical measurements plus 1.2cm (½ in).

Mark the Shoulder to Across Front minus 2.5cm (1 in) and the Shoulder to Across Back plus 2.5cm (1 in), but omit marking the shoulder to bust measurement and the shoulder to hem measurement. Imagine these marks as lines running across the folded fabric; the Shoulder to Waist mark, for example, will be the waistline. (02)

Place the horizontal measurements

Divide the Across Front and Across Back measurements by two and add 1.2cm (½ in) to each. Mark them along the relevant vertical mark, working from the centre fold, with a small cross. Divide the remaining horizontal measurements by four and add 5cm (2 in) to each. Mark these along the relevant line from the centre folds with a small cross. For example, mark the Waist divided by four plus 5cm (2 in) along the Shoulder to Waist mark. Along the hem, mark your Hip divided by four plus 5cm (2 in). Join the crosses with straight lines from the bustline to the hem. **(03)**

Shape the hemline

From the hemline cross, measure 5cm (2 in) up the side-seam line and place a mark. From this mark, draw a concave curve that grades down to roughly the middle of the hem. **(04)**

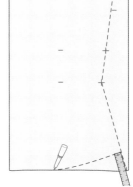

Shape the neck and shoulder

From the top corner of the centre folds, working along the shoulder seam, place a mark at 9cm (3½ in), and at a point that corresponds to your Back measurement divided by two plus 1.2cm (½ in).

Again from the top of the centre folds, this time working down the fold towards the hem, measure and place a mark at 9cm (3½ in). From the first mark along the shoulder seam (the 9cm/3½ in mark), draw a concave curve to the mark at the same distance down the centre folds. This is the neck hole; however, this is just for reference, as it will change a little further into the process. **(05)**

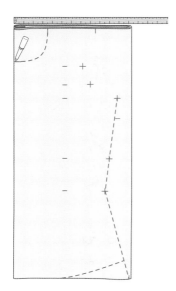

Shape the front armhole

From the cross at the bustline, draw a straight 5-cm (2-in) line towards the centre folds.

From the second mark made along the shoulder seam, draw a curved line that intercepts the cross at the Shoulder to Across Front and merges with the end of the 5-cm (2-in) line just drawn. This is the front armhole. (06)

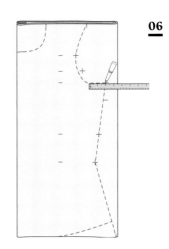

Shape the back armhole

From the cross at the bustline, measure downwards 5cm (2 in) and draw a straight line that runs parallel to the 5-cm (2-in) line above. From the second mark along the shoulder seam, draw a curve that intercepts the second cross and merges with the new 5-cm (2-in) line. Make sure that for the first 4cm (1½ in) of the curve, starting at the shoulder seam, the two lines merge into one. This is the back armhole.

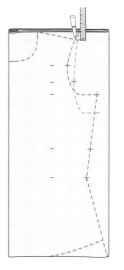

Finish the shoulder

From the top of the armholes, measure and mark 2cm (¾ in), then from this mark draw a sloping line to the top of the shoulder seam at the neck. This is to create the shoulder slope. (07)

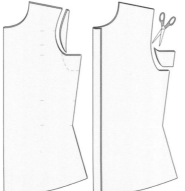

Cut out the front and back

You are now ready to cut. All the layers are cut in one go, but cut around all outer armhole lines first. Make a small notch in the side seam, through all the layers, at Underbust and Waist. Separate the front piece from the back piece.

Transfer the difference of the back armhole over from the front armhole and cut, then cut out the front armhole completely. (08)

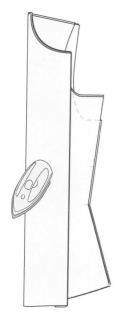

09

Fold the front darts

With both back and front folded with right sides together, place the front piece over the back piece, lining up the centre folds.

From the centre folds, measure and mark the Apex divided by two about midway down the length of the bodice. Use this mark as a guide for folding a dart crease that runs down the length of the bodice and which will appear on the front and back bodices. Press well. **(09)**

Separate the front and back pieces.

Fold the back darts

Working on the back pieces, place the two pieces with right sides together and pin along the centre-back crease. Use the iron to invert the dart crease that is projecting on the right side of the fabric (all dart creases should project towards the wrong side of the fabric).

Shape the back bodice darts

You will now need to mark and draw the darts on the left of the dart creases. At the Waist (and Underbust level), the dart is 1.2cm (½ in) wide. It tapers down to a point 18cm (7 in) towards the hemline, and tapers up to a point 18cm (7 in) above.

Fold and shape the bust darts

Now, working on the front piece, you will need to create bust dart folds from the side seam, before inverting these creases and drawing the darts. From the bustline, measure 10cm (4 in) down the side seam and mark.

From the highest point of the shoulder seam, mark the Shoulder to Bust measurement along the dart crease made earlier.

Fold across these two marks and press a crease that stops where this new crease meets the initial crease. (10)

Invert all the dart creases that are projecting on the right side of the fabric. On the front piece, you now have two sets of dart folds: the bodice front dart folds and the side bust dart folds.

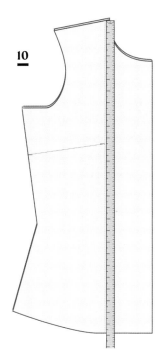

Shape the front bodice darts

Work on the front darts. The dart is 1.2cm (½ in) wide at the Waist. It tapers to a point 15cm (6 in) above the Waist at Underbust level, and tapers down to a point 18cm (7 in) below the Waist.

Shape the bust darts

Work on the bust dart fold, making sure the dart is on the fold and you are working to the left of the fold. The dart is 2.5cm (1 in) wide at the side seam (outer edge). Measure 4cm (1½ in) along the fold from the outer edge; at this point the dart is still 2.5cm (1 in) deep. From here, taper to a point 10cm (4 in) along the fold.

Sew the darts in the front and back pieces and press the darts outwards so that the dart seams go towards the side seams. Be careful not to remove the centre creases in both front and back pieces as you do so.

Sew the side seams: for a semi-fitted top

Lay the front piece on the back piece (both folded right sides together), making sure that the centre folds are aligned.

At this point you can simply line up the side seams, matching the notches, and sew with a 1.2-cm (½-in) seam. This will give a semi-fitted result.

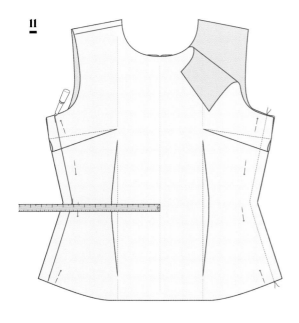

11

Mark the side seams: for a fitted top

Alternatively, for a more fitted top, line up the centre folds and make sure the notches at the side seams match up at the same level.

Place your hand over the fabric at waistline level and grip the side seam with one finger inserted between the layers. Pull on both layers gently, so that they are taut and flat. Pin in place around 5cm (2 in) inside the seam. Repeat this on the other side, and for both sides at Underbust level. These may not match up perfectly, and that is fine.

Match up and pin the side seams at bustline and hem level.

Starting from the centre crease, working towards your right-hand side, measure and mark your Bust, Underbust, Waist and Hip, each measurement divided by four, along the relevant body line.

Join the marks: this line is the seamline. (**11**)

Flip the bodice over so that the back is on top, and copy the seam allowance you made on the right-hand side. Sew along the lines drawn.

Shoulder seams

Sew the shoulder seam with a 1.2-cm (½-in) seam.

This is a good point to test the fit of the top, whether it is semi-fitted or fitted. To do this, you can put the top on and pin along the centre back crease (zip allowance fold).

Neck

Draw a non-conventional abstract neckline around the existing neck hole, using it as a guide. This neckline should be made up of mainly straight lines that meet at angled corners as pictured. Cut away the excess.(**12**)

13

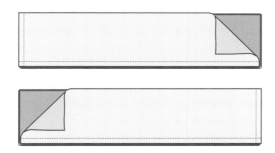

Collar

To cut the collar, measure the entire circumference of the neckline and cut out fabric as described in Pattern Pieces on page 30. Fold in half crossways (along the long side) and cut through the fold.

Use these two pieces as templates to cut out the same pieces in lining fabric and interfacing. (**13**)

Interfacing and lining

Affix the interfacing to the lining pieces. With the right sides of lining and collar together, pin the edges. Sew all along one short and one long raw edge, as pictured, with a 1.2-cm (½-in) seam.

Clip the corner section of the seam and understitch the seam to the lining. Press. Repeat for the second collar piece. (**14**)

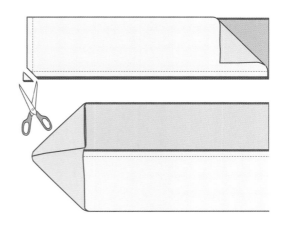

14

15

Attach the collar

With the right side of one collar facing the wrong side of the top's neckline, pin the raw edge of the collar to the neckline, starting at the centre-back fold. Make sure the sewn end of the collar exceeds the centre-back fold by 1.2cm (½ in), and create random pleats as you pin. (**15**) Repeat to add the second collar piece on the other side.

Sew with a 1.2-cm (½-in) seam. Trim and then zigzag or overlock the edge of the seam. Understitch the seam to the top.

Turn the two collar pieces over to the right side of the top, sew the short end of each collar along the corresponding zip allowance fold just as it exceeds the fold (this will help keep the collar and zip allowance fold as one piece when you sew in the zip). (**16**)

16

Zip

Sew in the zip (see page 16).

Hem

Hem the bottom edge with a double-turned hem (see page 15).

Sleeves

Follow the instructions for the sleeve block on pages 24–26, but the fabric width required will = Round Sleeve × 4 + 5cm (2 in). In step 3 omit the wrist marking, and in step 4 just join the first two crosses. Then place the head of your tape at the 'elbow length' cross and measure to the hem. Swivel the tape to mark this same measurement at regular intervals in a curve to the centre fold. This will create a curved extension to the hemline; the more you pivot out the wider will be the bell sleeve. From the 'elbow length' cross, draw a straight line to the end of your hem curve.

Angled-overlay pencil skirt

This project is a modern variation on a wardrobe staple: the classic knee-length pencil skirt. Make it in a fabric of your choice. For a more striking look, you can mix colours or textures. I have chosen African print, using a small design for the main skirt and a bolder print for the feature overlay. Both prints have the same colour palette, as I didn't want the print-on-print look to be jarring. You can also make the skirt at a shorter or longer length.

Measurements
(see pages 19–23)

Horizontal
Waist
Hip

Vertical
Waist to Hip: the distance between where the top of the skirt will sit and your hipline
Waist to Knee: the distance between where the top of the skirt will sit and your knee

Other
Apex

Materials
Cotton fabric for a skirt made in a single fabric:
(Waist to hemline) plus 6.25cm (2½ in) × Hip plus 2.3m (2½ yd)
Or main skirt:
Waist to hemline plus 6.25cm (2½ in) × Hip plus 46cm (18 in)
And overlay:
Hip plus 25cm (10 in) x 115cm (45 in)

And Waistband:
12.5cm (4 in) deep × Waist + 10cm (4 in) long
Matching thread
Zip: Use the longest length because you can always cut it down
Interfacing: 1m (1 yd) × 150cm (60 in) wide

Equipment
Basic sewing project equipment

Method

Cut out the skirt piece

Cut out a piece of fabric for the main part of the skirt using these measurements: Waist to hemline plus 6.25cm (2½ in) × Hip plus 46cm (18 in). Set the rest of the fabric aside: this will be used for the overlay and waistband.

African print fabric

If you choose to make the skirt in African print fabric, here are some handy little tips. Firstly, make sure you buy 100 per cent cotton because non cotton variety gets burnt easily with the iron and loses its brightness once washed. If it is your first time working freehand, go for a print that doesn't have an obvious repeat pattern, so there is no need to worry about pattern matching. African prints tend to be off the grain, so experience will be needed; however, there are hundreds of designs that are more friendly to first-timers, so don't be put off. Until you have understood how the technique works, you may find it difficult to align a pattern that is printed off the grain.

The prints usually look the same on both sides of the fabric, so it can be very difficult to tell the right side from the wrong side: look for the labelling along the selvedge, which will be printed on the right side, and then mark the wrong side of the fabric in several places before and after you cut out the pieces. (01)

<u>01</u>

African prints usually come with some branding stickers on them, and these can be a real pain. Avoid that section when cutting out if you can, or press the reverse of the fabric behind the sticker with a hot iron to heat the glue and allow you to peel off the sticker easily.

Hem

Decide which edge will form the hem; the opposite edge will be the waistline. Turn over a double fold towards the wrong side of the fabric to make the hem by first pressing over 1.2cm (½ in) and then 5cm (2 in). **(02)**

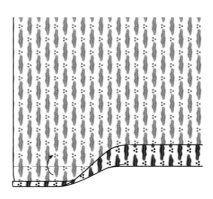

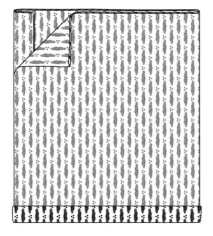

Centre front and centre back

Fold the fabric in half down the length, with the right side inside, to establish the centre front. At the open edge, fold 5cm (2 in) of both layers of the fabric towards the centre front; this fold is the centre back. The top raw edge is the waistline.

Bring the centre front over to meet the centre back: these folds – the centre folds – should line up exactly. **(03)**

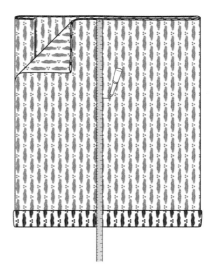

Working downward from the waistline, mark the Waist to Hip measurement with a small dash. This is the hipline. (**04**)

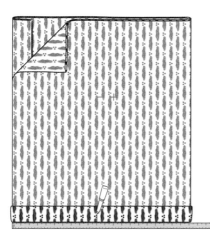

Shape the side seam

Measuring from the centre folds, mark a small cross along the hipline as follows: (Hip divided by four) plus 5cm (2 in). Measuring from the centre folds, mark a small cross along the waistline as follows: (Waist divided by four) plus 5cm (2 in).

Repeat the waistline formula along the hem if the skirt is around knee-length or beyond. If it is 12.5cm (5 in) or more above the knee, measure the circumference of the hem area on the wearer's body, divide by four and add 2.5cm (1 in), and then mark that along the hemline. (**05**)

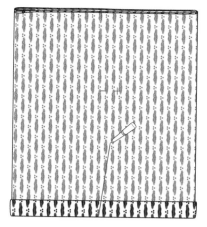

From the cross at the hemline, draw a straight line up half the distance to the hipline cross. (06)

From the cross at the waistline, draw a curve that intercepts the hipline cross and joins the top of the straight line previously drawn from the hem. (07)

Cut along this side seam line and snip a small notch at the hipline through all the layers.

07

08

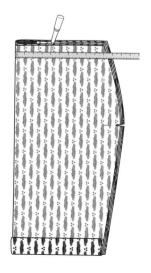

Darts

With the pieces still together from the cut. Divide your Apex by two and mark this distance from the centre folds. Fold along this point, which will form the centre line of the darts, and press the fold. (08)

Angled overlay

You will now use the front skirt piece as a template for cutting out the overlay. Unfold the front piece from the left edge of the waistline measure and mark 10cm (4 in) along the waistline. From the centre fold, along the hem, measure and mark 10cm (4 in) towards the right side seam. Place the overlay fabric, right side up, underneath the skirt piece, lining up the straight edge with the two marks made at the waist and hem, so that the overlay fabric is at an angle. (09) Make sure the slanted edge of the overlay fabric extends at least 25cm (10 in) beyond the hem. Pin in place.

Along the hem where the overlay fabric is, measure and mark 2.5cm (1 in) inside the side seam.

From the hem, along the slanted edge of the overlay fabric, measure and mark 25cm (1 in).

Join these two markings with a straight diagonal line. (10)

Cut along the lines you've just drawn with a 1.2cm (½ in) seam allowance and use your skirt as a template to cut out the rest of the overlay. (11). Notch the centre front at the waist and the hipline at the side seam.

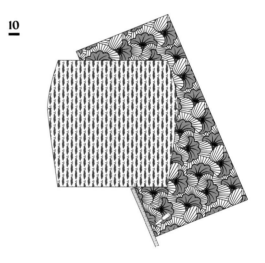

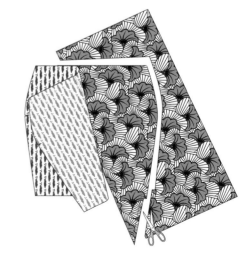

12

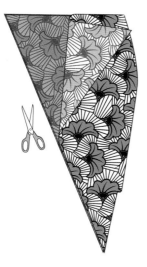

The overlay you just cut is the front piece, use this as a template to cut out lining and interfacing for the overlay, bear in mind that you will be fusing the interfacing to the lining piece. **(12)**

13

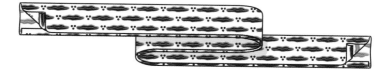

Waistband

To create the waistband, cut out a strip of fabric that measures 12.5cm (4 in) deep × Waist + 10cm (4 in) long. Fold and press the fabric in half along the length, with the right side outside. Fold and press 1.2cm (½ in) in towards the previous fold to create a clean edge on both sides of the waistband along the length. **(13)**

Now fold the waist band in half across the width, press. This is your centre front. Fold and press a 2.5cm (1 in) zip allowance fold along the open end, this is your centre back. Line the centre front up over the centre back and cut through the double folded edge opposite the centre folds; these are the side seams of the waistband. **(14)**

14

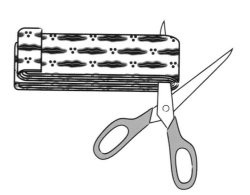

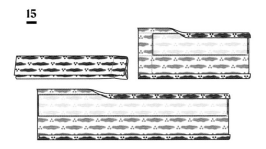

15

Use these pieces as a template to cut out interfacing for just half the depth of the waistband (so from the top folded edge of the waistband to the 1.2cm (½ in) under-fold). Fuse in place on the wrong side of the waistband (this will be the wrong side of the inner side of the waist band). (**15**)

Darts

Working on the front and back skirt pieces, make sure the dart creases you pressed earlier (Apex divided by two), are projecting on the wrong side of the fabric; use an iron to invert those that aren't. Work to the left of the crease, the darts are 1.2cm (½ in) deep at the waist and taper down 20cm (8 in) to a point along the crease. (**16**)

Sew all your darts and press them.

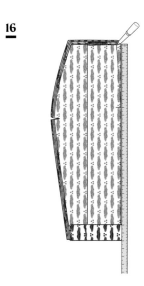

16

The overlay

Lay the overlay pieces together, right sides inside. Sew along the slanted edge with a 1.2cm (½ in) seam allowance, then top stitch the seam to the lining and press. (**17**)

With the right sides together again, sew the other diagonal edge that creates the overlay's point and the 2.5cm (1 in) straight line adjacent to it with a 1.2cm (½ in) seam allowance. Clip the corner to remove the bulk. (**18**) Turn out and press.

Place the overlay on the front piece matching up the centre front and hipline notches. Tack in place along the waistline and side seam, pushing the hem's turning out of the way when doing this.

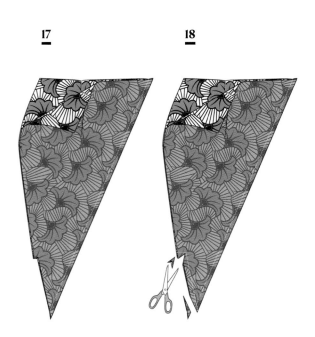

17   **18**

Angled-overlay Pencil Skirt

Attaching the waistband

Place the interfaced section of the waistband along the waist line of the skirt, making sure the centre folds are aligned. Sew with a 1.2cm (½ in) seam allowance. The fold you created in the waistband will help with this; align the raw edge of the waistband with the skirt's raw waistline and sew in the ditch of the fold. (19)

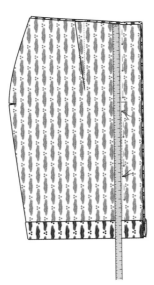

Working on the back skirt pieces, measure and mark 22.5cm (9 in) and 25cm (10 in) from the waist along the centre back creases (the fold of the zip allowance). The 22.5-cm (9-in) point serves as a guide as to where your zip stops.

Decide how high up you want the slit of your skirt to be and mark this along the centre back, measuring up from the hem.

Sew the back pieces together along the zip allowance fold, from the 25cm (10 in) point to the slit height. (20)

Attach the back waistband as previously, making sure the zip allowance folds (centre back) are aligned.

Side seams

Pin the centre back seam together completely (some of it is already sewn), lay the front over the back piece, aligning the centre folds and matching the side seams, and pin together about 5cm (2 in) inside the edge. The waistband and hem must be unfolded.

Along the waist, mark the waist divided by four, measuring from the centre folds. Do the same with the hip measurement along the hip line and again with the waist measurement along the hem (unless you took the actual measurement of the hem circumference area, in which case divide that by four). This will give you a very fitted skirt; if you would like some ease, I suggest adding 0.6cm (0.25 in) after dividing by four. Join these marks with smooth curved lines. Copy this seam allowance to the other side. Sew along the lines. (**21**)

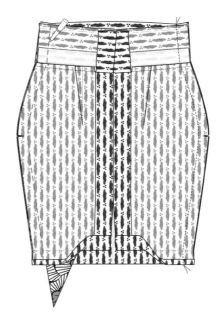

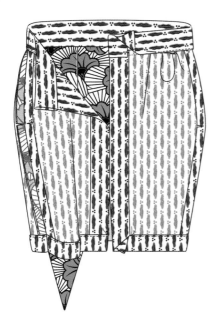

Test the fit; once you are happy, you may trim down the side seam to 1.2cm (½ in). I usually leave it because my weight tends to fluctuate so I can release the seams as much as I like. Zig zag or overlock the seams (see page 11) and press open.

Fold the waistband back down, sandwiching the joining seam of the skirt waist and the waist band in-between the folded edge of the waistband. Pin in place and neatly hand sew making sure your stitching doesn't go through to the right side. (**22**)

Refold the hem and sew along the entire circumference, 3mm (⅛ in) inside the fold.

Insert your zip (see page 16 or 18, depending on your zip style).

Child's denim dress

This is a cute way to rework the original seams and shape of a pair of jeans into a simple dress for a little princess. The project will work with any pair of trousers, not just jeans.

Measurements
(see pages 19–23)
When taking measurements, add some ease because you're making for a child.

Horizontal
Back
Chest

Other
Shoulder Seam (SS): from the centre of the shoulder to the desired hem line
Armhole (AH): wrap the tape around the arm socket giving enough room for free movement
Round Sleeve (RS)
Round Elbow (RE)
Elbow Length (EL)
Sleeve Length (SL)

Materials
Old straight-legged jeans, preferably in a large size
Matching thread
Bias binding: 1.2cm (½ in) wide
Embellishments
Zip

Equipment
Basic sewing project equipment

Method

Prepare the denim

Unpick one of the back pockets of the jeans and set this aside.

Cut off the legs of the jeans at crotch level. Unpick the seams of the legs and press. (01)

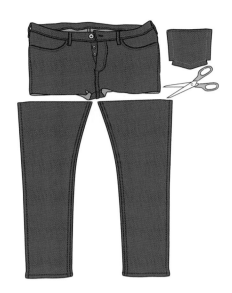

01

Prepare the front and back of the dress

Sew the two front leg pieces together, with right sides facing, along the outer leg seams. Repeat for the back legs, but use a tacking stitch.

Fold the pieces along the sewn seams, with right sides facing. Lay the front leg block of fabric over the back leg block, aligning the seams. (02)

The top of the jeans leg at thigh level will form the hem of the dress, because we will use the fluted cut to create the shape of the dress. Turn the fabric blocks so the hem is at the bottom, then measure upwards from the hem as follows: Shoulder to Hem plus 4cm (1.5 in). Draw a horizontal straight line at this point. (03)

Cut along the line: this is now the shoulder seam. Set the offcuts aside to use for the sleeves. (04)

02

03

04

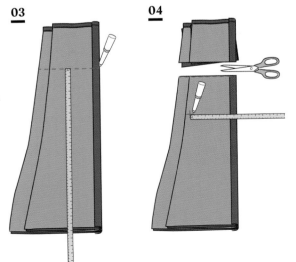

Create the shape of the dress

Place the head of the tape measure at the shoulder seam, and mark the chest line as follows: (AH divided by two) plus 1.2cm (½ in).

Working from the centre of the body, measure along the chest line and mark with a small cross as follows: (Chest divided by four) plus 4cm (1½ in).

From that point, measure the distance straight down to the hem and make a note of it. Keeping the head of the tape measure at the cross, pivot towards the outer edge, marking the hemline depth at intervals as you go. Continue until you hit the edge. (05)

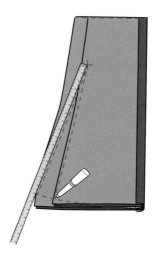

05

Neck and armholes

From the chest-line cross, draw a straight line to the end of the curved base on both the front and back leg pieces.

Along the shoulder seam, measure and mark from the centre front and centre back outwards as follows: back divided by two. Add 5cm (2 in) and mark to establish the outer point of the shoulder.

From that point, measure out the Shoulder Seam length towards the neck. From the top centre-folds corner, measure and mark 7.5cm (3 in) down along the centre seams. Draw a neckline curve that connects the two markings. (06)

From the second mark along the shoulder seam (outer shoulder), draw an armhole curve to the chest-line cross.

06

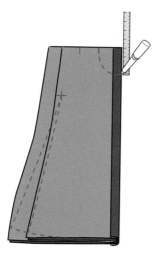

Measure and mark 1.2cm (½ in) down the armhole from the shoulder. From this point draw a straight line that slopes to the top of the neckline. **(07)**

Cut along the lines.

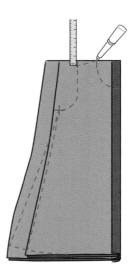

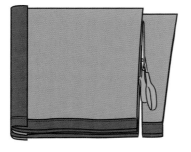

08

Sleeves

Work with the off cuts from the trouser legs. Fold them right sides inside along the seam line; you will find that the piece made from the back leg panels is longer than the piece made from the front leg. Cut the larger piece down to the same size as the smaller piece. **(08)**

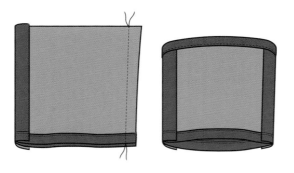

09

With the right sides inside, sew the seam opposite the sewn seam with a 1.2cm (½ in) seam allowance to create a tube. Then hem the edge opposite the original trouser hem with a double turned 1.2cm (½ in) hem. **(09)**

Child's Denim Dress

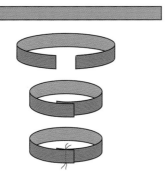

10

Measure out a length of elastic that sits comfortably around the top of the child's arm, add 2.5cm (1 in) and cut four the same length. Overlap the ends of each piece by 2.5cm (1 in) and sew a running stitch 6mm (¼ in) inside each cut end of the overlapped elastic. This will create four loops of elastic. (10)

Find the mid-point of the elastic on either side, mark with a chalk so that it's easily identified, then pin each mark to the side seams of the sleeve, positioning the elastic just below the hem's inner edge. (11)

11

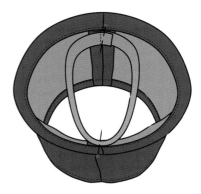

12

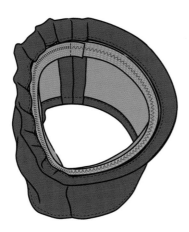

Stretch the elastic to fit the space between the pins as you sew. Sew with a wide zig zag stitch along the centre of the elastic, all the way around. This will create gathers. (12)

Pocket, side seams and shoulder seams

Position the back pocket you removed earlier on the front of the dress. Sew a double line of stitching around the sides and bottom to secure it in place. (13)

With the right sides together, sew the side seams of the dress with a 1.2-cm (½-in) seam.

With the right sides together, sew the shoulder seams with a 1.2-cm (½-in) seam.

Finish the neck and hem

Unpick the centre-back seam and use bias binding to finish the neckline (see page 14).

13

14

Insert the sleeves

Hem the bottom edge with a double-turned hem (see page 15).

Turn the dress inside out and the sleeves right-side out. With the right sides together, line up the top edge of the seam with the bottom edge of the armhole, matching up the side seams, and aligning the shoulder seam with the centre sleeve seam. Sew with a 1.2-cm (½-in) seam from 2.5cm (1 in) before the side seam to 2.5cm (1 in) after it. (14)

Zip

Insert a zip (see page 16 or 18, depending on what type of zip you are using).

Sassy tutu skirt

T his is one of those easy makes that has huge impact. It can be made with trousers of any fabric, but I have made mine from a pair of not-too-big jeans because I like the playful outcome that can be dressed up or dressed down. Why not try starting with some trousers made in a block-coloured traditional suiting or crepe fabric, teamed with a matching coloured tulle for a more formal look. Either way, this skirt is sure to leave a lasting impression.

Measurements (see pages 19–23)

Note that for the purposes of this project, the definitions of the horizontal and vertical measurements are different to those used in other projects.

Horizontal

Waist: the circumference that corresponds to where you want the top of the skirt to sit (not necessarily your natural waist)
Hip: circumference of hips

Vertical

Waist to Hip: the distance between where the top of the skirt will sit and your hipline
Waist to hem: total skirt length from top of the skirt to the hemline

Other

Jeans Hip: jeans' circumference at hipline (see 'Resize Jeans for the Desired Waistline')
Jeans Waist: jeans' circumference at waistline (see 'Resize Jeans for the Desired Waistline')
Hem circumference: circumference of bottom of upper skirt
Hem 1: length of upper skirt
Hem 2: overall length of skirt

Pattern pieces for sassy tutu skirt

Lower skirt:
(Hem circumference divided by 6.28, rounded up to a whole number) × 3 = lower skirt first radius
(Hem 2 minus hem 1) plus 2.5cm (1 in) = lower skirt second radius

Lining:
Hem circumference divided by 3.14 = lining first radius
(Hem 1 plus hem 2) minus 5cm (2 in) = lining second radius

Materials

Jeans: a pair of jeans that fits round your waist
Tulle: 8m (8¾ yd)
Lining: 2nd radius × 2
Matching thread

Equipment

Basic sewing project equipment

Method

Prepare the denim

Unpick the waistband from the jeans, leaving the belt loops attached to the waistband. Cut off the legs as close to the crotch as possible. Set aside the legs and waistband. (01)

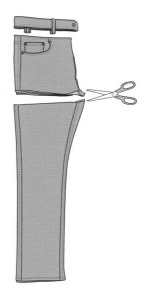

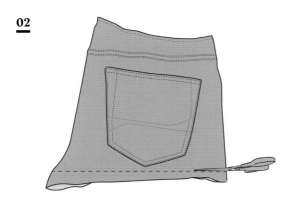

Fold the jeans in half, and draw a line across the bottom edge to make it straight. Push the pocket bags up out of the way and cut along this line. This will get rid of the crotch area. (02)

Upper skirt

Unfold the jeans and place the side seams on top of each other so that the front is folded in half on one side, and the back is folded in half on the opposite side.

Starting from the centre-back waist, draw a straight line down the centre-back seam. Cut along this line and pin the seam with a 1.2-cm (½-in) seam allowance.

You may find that the waist seam is higher at the centre back. Cut it level with the front waistline. (03)

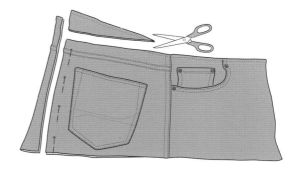

Establish the upper skirt's waistline

Decide whether you want a high-waisted skirt or whether you want the waistline to sit lower down. I am making a high-waisted version because I prefer the silhouette. Wherever this waistline falls, it corresponds to the Waist measurement.

Resize jeans for the desired waistline

Measure the waist of the jeans; subtract your waist measurement from this, divide the sum by four and mark this along the waist from the sewn line in towards the centre.

Near the side seam measure and mark your Waist to Hip measurement: this is your hipline. Measure the jeans' circumference at this level, note it down as Jeans Hip.

Subtract your hip measurement from the Jean Hip and divide the sum by four. Mark this at hip level, from the sewn line at the side seam in towards the centre.

Side and centre-back seams

Draw a curved line that connects the two side-seam markings, and then continue straight down to the hem. This line is your new side seam.

Turn the jeans over and copy the new seam allowance to the other side of the skirt.

Sew the side seams. Sew the centre-back seam with a 1.2-cm (½-in) seam allowance. Test the fit, and once you're happy, measure the circumference of the hem.

Lower skirt: tutu effect

Cut three pieces of tulle fabric to the following dimensions: second radius × second radius.

Fold each piece in half along the 'width' and in half again along the 'length'.

Place the tape measure at the corner that has only folded edges and no open edges, then use it as a 'compass' and pivot to mark the first and second radiuses. Cut along these lines. Repeat for each piece. (04)

Lining

Note that only the lower tulle skirt is lined.

Cut the lining fabric to the following dimensions: lining second radius × lining second radius.

Fold each piece in half along the 'width' and in half again along the 'length'.

Place the tape measure at the corner that has only folded edges and no open edges, then use it as a 'compass' and pivot to mark the first and second lining radiuses.

Cut along these lines and set the lining aside.

Waistband

Open the jeans waistband (do not unpick the ends) and fold it in half with the right sides together. Measure the length of the waistband and subtract your Waist measurement from this, then divide the sum by two. Measuring from the fold, mark this distance with a line that runs parallel to the fold.

Sew along the marked line and cut off the excess seam allowance. (05)

05

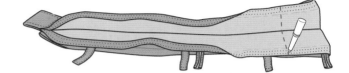

Join the lower skirt

Open the tulle circles, place them on top of each other, and sew two rows of gathering stitches around the first-radius edge.

Gather the tulle into the hem of the upper skirt, making sure the gathers are evenly spread and pinning in place with right sides together. Sew the lower skirt to the upper skirt with a 1.2-cm (½-in) seam allowance.

Insert the lining

Now pin the top of the lining to the hem of the upper skirt, with the right side of the lining to the right side of the skirt and the tulle sandwiched in-between. Sew with a 1.2-cm (½-in) seam. Hem the lining with a narrow, double-turned hem.

06

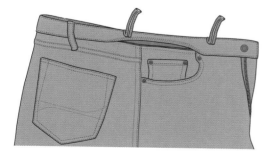

Apply the waistband

Sandwich the waistline edge of the upper skirt in the original waistband of the jeans. Sew along the original seamline, matching the centre-back seams. (06) Re-sew the bottom ends of the belt loops to the skirt along the original seam lines.

WALNUT ST.
COLLEGE HILL
CENTRE SQUARE
GLENDON
WEST EASTO
EASTON
ISLAND PAR
NORTH MAI
SOUTH MAIN
ALPHA
OAKLAND PARK
BETHLEHEM
BETH. - NAZARETH
NAZARETH

Pencil dress refit

The primary aim of this project is to demonstrate how you can add another fabric to alter the length and overall look of a dress. I started out with an oversized minidress with side peplums that I didn't really fancy. I really liked its elegant, pleated neckline detail. In keeping with that elegance, I decided to extend the dress to a midi length with some sheer organza fabric. I have also completely refitted the dress so it is the exact size I need it to be. You may decide to start with a dress that already fits you perfectly – in which case you can skip steps 1 to 6.

Measurements (see pages 19–23)

Horizontal
Bust
Waist
Hips

Vertical
Shoulder to Waist
Shoulder to Hip
Desired length of dress

Other
New skirt waist formula:
(Waist circumference of the existing skirt minus your Waist) divided by four = new skirt waist
New skirt hip:
(Hip circumference of the existing skirt minus your Hip) divided by four = new skirt hip
New bodice front:
(Bust circumference of the existing bodice minus your Bust) divided by four = new bodice bust
(Waist circumference of the existing bodice minus your Waist) divided by four = new bodice waist
Organza skirt panel:
Width (horizontal measurement) of skirt offcut plus 2.5cm (1 in) × (depth – the length you want to extend the dress by – plus 5cm/ 2 in)

Materials
Oversized sleeveless minidress with a pencil skirt (that is to say, in a size that is bigger than your normal dress size)
Organza: about 1m (1 yd), depending on the length you are trying to create
Matching thread

Equipment
Basic sewing project equipment

Method

Place vertical measurements

Turn the dress inside out. If there is a lining, push that up out of the way because you will be working on the skirt itself first of all.

Take the Shoulder to Waist measurement minus 1.2cm (½ in) and place this parallel with the waist seam to indicate the new waistline.

Mark the Shoulder to Hip measurement. (**01**)

I needed to remove the side peplums on my dress, so I unpicked the waist seam starting and stopping about 5cm (2 in) from the zip. It you don't have anything at the waist to remove, you can leave the waist seam in place.

Mark the new skirt waist, measuring from the sewn line in towards the centre of the skirt.

Mark the new skirt hip, working from the sewn line at hip level. (**02**)

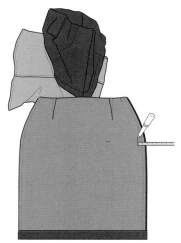

Side seams

Unpick the hem around the side seam area only. Measure in 2.5cm (1 in) from the sewn line. (**03**)

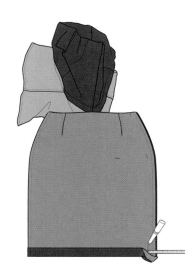

Join the first two marks at the side (waistline and new skirt hip) with a curved line, then extend the line to the mark at the hem. This forms the new side seam.

Copy the seam on the other side of the dress. (04)

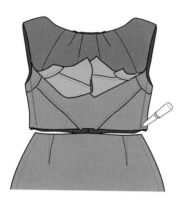

Adjust the bodice to fit

Measure the bust of the dress bodice (the bustline is always the base of the armhole). If the dress has a lining, lift it out of the way so that the bustline seam of the dress is exposed.

Mark the new bodice bust, working along the bustline from the sewn line.

Mark the new bodice waist in the same way. Connect the two markings with a straight line. Copy this seam allowance to the other side. (05)

Adjust the lining to fit

If your dress is lined, copy the seam allowance on to the lining on both side seams. (Notice that I haven't unpicked the waist seam of the lining because the peplum was only fitted into the outer dress.) (06)

Complete the seams

Sew all the new seam lines and you should have a perfectly fitted dress. This method is also an effective way of making a shop-bought dress fit you like a bespoke dress.

Chop off the bottom of the dress

To extend the length of the dress, decide where you want the panel to go, measure from the hem to that point, and mark at intervals until there is a horizontal line across the dress. Cut along the line.

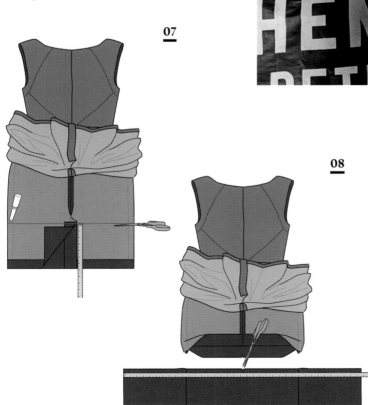

07

08

(My organza panel starts below the back hem vent, so rather than joining the seams of the panel down the centre back, I will turn a narrow hem and leave it open ended.) (07)

Find the centre front of the two raw edges you just cut (at the bottom of the dress and at the top of the cut-off piece of the skirt) and notch. Measure the width of the skirt offcut. (08)

Attach the panel

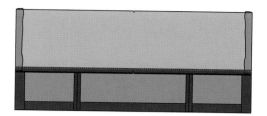

09

Cut out an organza panel (see Pattern Pieces). Notch the centre along both edges of the width.

Match the bottom side's notch with the centre notch of the skirt offcut. With right sides together, sew with a 1.2-cm (½-in) seam. **(09)**

Press the seam towards the hem of the dress and understitch (see page 13) to the original skirt piece to prevent the seam rolling into view.

10

Attach the panel to the dress, making sure the centre front notches match. Press the seam towards the waist and understitch to the original dress. **(10)**

Refit the lining

If the dress is lined and you have used sheer fabric to create the panel, you will need to cut down the lining so that it doesn't show behind the panel. This is easy: simply follow the process for cutting off the bottom of the dress. Turn a double hem to finish the hem of the lining.

Sleeves

To add long sleeves, unpick the seam around the armhole to remove the armhole facing, but do not press it.

Cut out your desired sleeve style (see pages 24–26) and sew the side seam. Because it is a sheer fabric, I have used a French seam (see page 10).

Hem the sleeve with a 1.2-cm (½-in) double-rolled hem. Insert the sleeve into the armhole (see page 27).

If the dress is lined, reattach the bodice lining around the armhole, matching the side and shoulder seam, and hand-sew it neatly to the dress fabric with the sleeve seam sandwiched in between.

Asymmetric peplum top

If you know me, then you know I love a peplum, as the possibilities with them are endless. They are über-feminine, and a well-fitted peplum top or dress can really transform, flatter or accentuate most body types.

Measurements (see pages 19–23)

Horizontal
Back
Across Front
Across Back
Bust
Underbust
Waist
Hip

Vertical
Shoulder to Across Front
Shoulder to Across Back
Shoulder to Bust
Shoulder to Underbust
Shoulder to Waist
Shoulder to hem

Other
Apex

Materials
Cotton fabric:
Bodice, including self-lining: about Bust measurement × 3 and Shoulder to Waist wide
Peplum and ruffles, including self-lining: about 2.75–3.6m (3–4 yd)
Matching thread
Zip: use the longest length because you can always cut it down

Pattern pieces for asymmetric peplum top
Peplum formula:
(Waist × 2, divided by 3.14) divided by two = first radius
(Shoulder to hem minus Shoulder to Waist) plus first radius = second radius
Peplum fabric:
Second radius plus 5cm (2 in) × second radius plus 5cm (2 in)
Bodice fabric:
Bust plus 35.5cm (14 in) × (Shoulder to Waist) plus 2.5cm (1 in)

Equipment
Basic sewing project equipment

Method

Fold the fabric

Press every fold definitely. Fold the fabric in half with right sides together, so the fold line runs down the length. The folded edge forms the centre front of the bodice. On the open side opposite the centre front, fold in 2.5cm (1 in) down the entire length on both edges, for the zip allowance at the centre back of the bodice. Press these folds well. The top edge of the folded fabric piece will be the shoulder of the bodice and the bottom edge will be the waistline seam. At the centre back, make sure the raw edge and the folded zip allowance edge are aligned, then bring the centre-front fold over to align with the centre back. These are the centre folds.

Place the vertical body measurements for front and back

Measuring down from the shoulder seam edge, somewhere near the middle of the folded block of fabric, mark the vertical body measurements with small horizontal lines but omit the Shoulder to Bust and Shoulder to Hem. The measurements are as follows: 23cm (9 in) from the top edge (for the bust line); and all other vertical measurements plus 1.2cm (½ in).

Place the horizontal body measurements for front and back

Now visualise these marked vertical measurements as lines running horizontally across the fabric; the 23-cm (9-in) mark is the bustline. Each of these marked vertical measurements has a corresponding horizontal measurement that creates the shape of the bodice.

Measuring out from the centre folds, divide the Across Front by two and add 2.5cm (1 in); mark along the Across Front line with a dot. Repeat this for the Across Back measurement but only add 1.2cm (½ in) to the Shoulder to Across Back rather than 2.5cm (1 in).

Divide each of the other horizontal body measurements (Back, Bust, Underbust, Waist, Hips) by four and add 5cm (2 in). Mark these along the relevant horizontal line, working inwards from the centre folds, by making a small cross. For example, divide the Waist by four and add 5cm (2 in), marking this along the Shoulder to Waist horizontal line. (01)

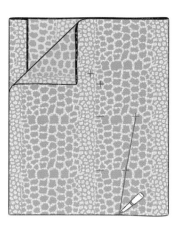

Create the bodice shape

Join the crosses with straight lines.

Create the neckline and armholes

From the cross at the bustline, draw a 5-cm (2-in) straight line towards the centre folds. Working from the centre folds, along the shoulder seam, mark 9cm (3½ in) and your Back measurement divided by two, plus 1.2cm (½ in). Measure 9cm (3½ in) down the centre folds from the shoulder edge. To create the neck, draw a scoop that joins the two 9-cm (3½-in) marks.

02

To create the front armhole, draw a curved line from the second mark along the shoulder seam: it intercepts the Across Front dot and merges with the end of the 5-cm (2-in) line drawn at bustline level. Repeat this step for the back armhole, but this time intercept the Across Back dot and make sure the first 4cm (1½ in) of the curve, starting from the shoulder seam, merges with the front armhole. To create the shoulder slope, measure and mark 2cm (¾ in) down from the top of the armholes. From this point, draw a line up to the neck/ shoulder point. This forms the shoulder seam. (02)

Cut out the front and back

Cut around the lines through all the layers, making sure to cut only the outer markings in the armhole area. Make a notch in the side seam, through all the layers, at the Waist and Underbust levels.

Separate the front and back pieces and cut out the front armhole.

Pin the back pieces together along the zip allowance crease, so that you can unfold it as one piece. Unfold the bodice front, then place it over the unfolded back bodice with the right sides together. Measure and mark 9cm (3½ in) down one of the armholes, then draw a curve from here to the neckline on the opposite side to create the asymmetric style line. Cut this out through all layers. **(03)**

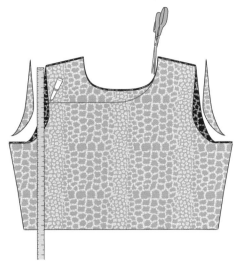

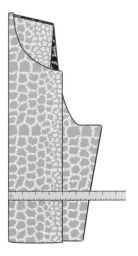

Dart folds, front and back bodice

Fold the front and back bodice pieces again. Place the front piece over the back piece, lining up the centre folds as previously. Working from the centre folds, measure and mark your Apex divided by two, locating it about midway down the length of the top. Use this mark as a guide for folding a dart crease that runs down the length of the bodice, to provide darts for front and back. **(04)**

Separate the front and back bodice pieces.

Shape the back darts

Working on the back bodice pieces, use the iron to invert the crease that is projecting on the right side of the fabric (all final dart creases need to project on the wrong side of the fabric).

Mark and draw the darts on the left of the dart creases. The dart is 1.2cm (½ in) wide at the Waist and tapers to a point 20cm (8 in) above it.

05

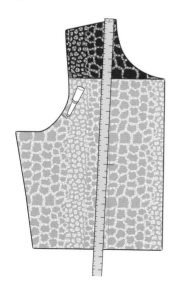

Shape the front darts

The darting for the front of the bodice is going to be sewn as one continuous dart that combines an armhole dart and front-bodice dart. However, not all sections of the dart will be drawn on the fabric. From the highest point of the shoulder seam, measure and mark the Shoulder to Bust plus 1.2cm (½in) along the dart crease made initially. Find the deepest part of the armhole curve and mark it (some sections of the armhole are more of a slightly bent line than a true curve, but what you are looking for is the deepest part of the true curve in the armhole). **(05)**

Fold and press what should be a diagonal crease connecting these two marks.

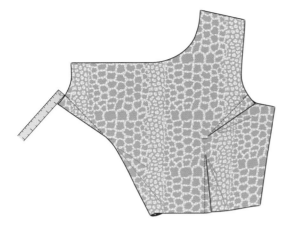

The armhole dart is 2.5cm (1 in) wide at the armhole (when in the diagonal fold of the dart, you will likely find that the armhole edges don't match up, but this is fine). From that mark, the dart slants 7.5cm (3 in) down towards the fold. Do not taper this line to a point at the fold: stop 6mm (¼ in) short of the fold.

The front-bodice section of this dart is 1.2cm (½ in) deep at the Waist, and 4cm (1.5 in) deep at the Underbust. From here it tapers to a point 15cm (6 in) above the waist along the fold. If you find that the top of this dart is not at least 1.2cm (½ in) below the crease interception point (bust point), then adjust the dart length until that happens. It is absolutely fine if it is more than 1.2cm (½ in) below the bust point. (06)

Peplum

Cut the peplum fabric (see Pattern Pieces).
Fold the fabric in half with the right sides facing each other, then fold in half again along the folded edge. From the corner with only folded edges, using your tape as a 'compass', pivot and mark the first and second radiuses. Cut out the peplum with a 1.2-cm (½-in) seam allowance at the waistline edge.

Unfold the piece once to form a semi circle; measure and mark 7.5cm (3 in) up from the hemline edge along one of the folded edges. From the mark, draw a gently curving line to finish at the bottom end of the centre crease on the semi circle. Cut along the line.

07

Now take the newly shortened folded edge and line it up over the centre crease, as if creating an 8th of the circle with just that section. Finger-press a crease, then carefully put your scissors in between both layers of the new crease and cut only one layer of fabric. (07)

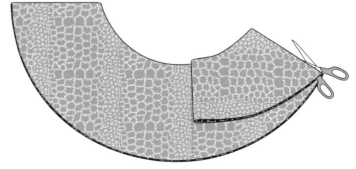

This will give you a circle with an opening. This opening is going to be where your zip is inserted at the side of the top. Use this as a template to cut out self-lining in the same material.

Neckline ruffle

Measure the entire neckline of the top. Repeat the peplum process to make the neckline ruffle using the neckline measurement in place of the waist measurement. When working out the second radius, determine how long you want the ruffle to be and use that instead of Shoulder to hem minus Shoulder to Waist.

Once cut, unfold the piece once to make a semi circle, and measure and mark 6.25cm (2½ in) up from the hemline edge along one of the folded edges. From the mark, draw a gently curving line that ends at the bottom end of the centre crease on the semi circle. Cut along the line.

Unfold and use this as a template to cut a lining in the same fabric.

Sew the front and back darts

Sew the back darts.

Sew the front darts. Start from the armhole, following the 7.5-cm (3-in) line you drew, and when you reach the end of it, begin to grade the sewing line downward until you are 3mm (¹/₈ in) from the fold. Carry on 3mm (¹/₈ in) from the fold until you reach the exact point where the dart creases intercept each other. The easiest way to achieve this is to use your hand to control the machine manually from 1.2cm (½ in) before the interception point, as it allows you to be very precise. At that point, with the needle down, raise the presser foot and pivot the fabric so that you are now working on the front-bodice portion of the dart; wiggle the fabric around to release any puckers before putting the foot back down. Manually control the machine for a couple of stitches, then continue at 3mm (¹/₈ in) from the fold until you come to the drawn dart line. Continue along the dart line until the dart is completely sewn.

Side seams

There may now be a step in the armhole from where the armhole edges didn't align when creating the dart creases. To realign the armhole, fold the front in half so that the armholes are aligned, then redraw the armhole curve to remove the step, cut along the drawn curve and if this has cut into the dart at all, secure the beginning of the dart with a back and forth stitch.

Place the front piece over the back piece with the right sides facing each other. Make sure that the centre creases are lined up and the notches at the side seams are at the same level.

08

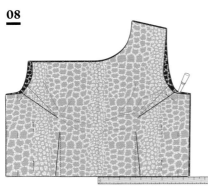

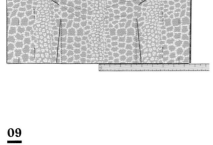

09

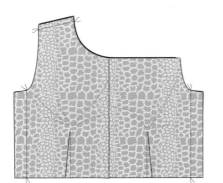

Place your hand over the fabric at waistline level and grip the side seam with one finger inserted between the layers. Pull on both layers gently so that they are taut and flat. Pin in place around 5cm (2 in) inside the seam. Repeat on the other side, and for both sides at Underbust level. These may not match up perfectly, and that is fine. Match up and pin the side seams at bustline and hem level.

Now take the Bust, Underbust, Waist and Hip measurements, divide them by four and mark these along the relevant levels, marking from the centre crease outwards only on the right-hand side. (08)

Join the marks: this line is the seam line. Flip the other seam of the bodice over so that the back is on top, and copy the seam allowance you made on to this side. (09)

Sew along the lines made, but in the side seam where the top has a complete shoulder, use a wide length stitch as this is only tacking. Sew the shoulder seam with a 1.2-cm (½-in) seam. Zigzag or overlock the edges of the seam. Press the seam open.

Unpick the basting stitches; you are only unpicking the side seam and not the shoulder seam. The crease you made when pressing this seam open will be where the zip is inserted.

Sew the centre back seam together along the zip allowance fold because the zip will be inserted in the side.

Armholes

Bias-bind both armholes (see page 15).

Attach the peplum and ruffle

Work on the peplum: place the peplum and lining with right sides together (they are cut from the same fabric). Sew around the outer edge of the circle with a 1.2-cm (½-in) seam, clip the seam, and understitch the seam to the lining. Turn the peplum right side out. Repeat the process to make the neckline ruffle.

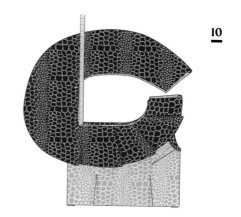

10

Work on the neckline. Turn the bodice wrong-side out and pin the shorter side of the ruffle around the shoulder seam area. The right side of the ruffle needs to be facing the wrong side of the neckline. Randomly pleat the ruffle as you pin it along the rest of the neckline. As you pass the cut shoulder, leave out 15cm (6 in) of the ruffle. (**10**)

Notch the beginning and end of the 15cm (6 in) with a 1.2-cm (½-in) snip. (**11**)

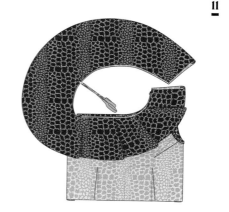

11

Unpin the area around the 15cm (6 in) left-out ruffle so that you can turn it to have the right sides facing, and sew from notch to notch. Do not envelope the ruffle in between the seam before sewing. Turn right-side out and you should have a nice clean edge. Press this and re-pin the unpinned neckline. Sew with a 1.2-cm (½-in) seam and understitch the seam to the bodice. (**12**)

Pin the peplum to the bodice waistline, creating random pleats as you pin. Sew with a 1.2-cm (½-in) seam and zigzag or overlock the seam.

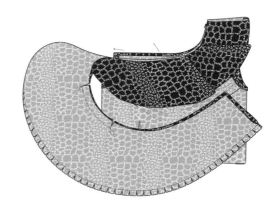

12

Zip

Zigzag stitch the raw ends of the peplum to the zip seam allowance. Inset the zip into the open side seam using the crease as a guide (see page 18).

Strapless wrap dress

The his darling little dress can look dramatically different depending on your choice of fabric and the length of the dress. I have chosen a shirt fabric and a mid length, suitable for a summer afternoon soirée. How about making it in a luxury silk satin at a maxi length, for an ultra-glamorous version? The construction uses a firm lining to help support the bodice, with channels to contain boning that will uphold the strapless design.

Measurements (see pages 19–23)

Horizontal
Back
Across Front
Across Back
Bust
Underbust
Waist

Vertical
Shoulder to Across Front
Shoulder to Across Back
Shoulder to Bust
Shoulder to Overbust
Shoulder to Underbust
Shoulder to Waist
Shoulder to Hem

Other
Apex

Pattern pieces for strapless wrap dress
Bodice:
Bust plus 38cm (15 in) ×
Shoulder to Waist
Flared skirt formula:
(Waist measurement plus
25.5cm/ 10 in) divided by 3.14 =
first radius
First radius plus (Shoulder to
hem minus Shoulder to Waist)
plus 2.5cm (1 in) = second
radius
Fabric quantity for skirt:
(Second radius × 2) × second
radius plus 2.5cm (1 in)

Belt:
(Waist × 2) × 20cm (8 in)

Materials
Dress fabric: 3.6m (4 yd) ×
150cm (60 in) wide
Calico (for templates): 1m (1 yd)
Bodice lining (e.g. polyester
cotton, in a colour that will not
show through the dress fabric):
1m (1 yd)
Fusible interfacing: 1m (1 yd)
Matching thread
Plastic boning: 2m (2 yd)

Equipment
Basic sewing project equipment

Method

Prepare the skirt fabric

Fold the fabric in half crossways (along the width). Next, bring the lower end of the fold up to lie 2.5cm (1 in) inside the adjacent edge. This will create a bias fold.

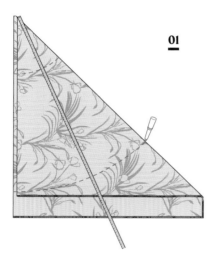

<u>01</u>

Cut out the skirt

Using the formula in Pattern Pieces, cut out the fabric for the flared skirt. Use the head of the tape measure as a 'compass' and pivot to mark the first and second radius from the pointed corner.

Cut out the skirt, with a 1.2-cm (½-in) seam allowance at the waistline. (01)

Prepare the bodice templates

Fold the template fabric in half crossways (along the width), with right sides together. This fold is the centre front.

The side opposite the centre-front fold is the centre back. Fold over a 2.5-cm (1-in) zip allowance on both edges towards the centre front. Bring the centre front over to line up with the centre back. These are the centre folds.

Place the vertical body measurements

Work out the following: (Shoulder to Overbust) minus 1.2cm (½ in). Find this measurement on the tape measure, and place it at the top edge of the block of fabric. For instance, if the measurement is 14cm (5½ in), this position on the tape would be level with the top edge.

With the tape in place, measure and mark the following vertical measurements: 23cm (9 in), Shoulder to Underbust, and Shoulder to Waist. If you imagine lines running horizontally at these points, these equate to the style line of the strapless bodice, the underbust line, and the waistline.

Place the horizontal body measurements

At the vertical reference points you have just made, mark the corresponding horizontal measurements for the Bust, Underbust and Waist with a small cross as follows: (measurement divided by four) plus 5cm (2 in). **(02)**

Join the crosses with straight lines to establish the side of the bodice.

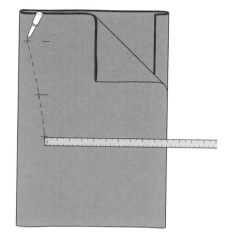

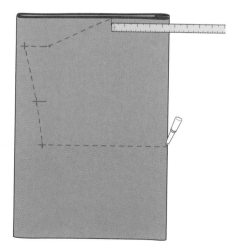

Start shaping the bodice templates

From the cross marking the style line of the bodice (the first vertical reference mark – the 23-cm/ 9-in one), draw a horizontal 5-cm (2-in) line towards the centre back.

Working from the centre folds along the top edge, mark as follows: (Apex divided by two) plus 1.2cm (½ in). Connect this to the end of the horizontal line (this line will be diagonal).

Draw a horizontal line at the waistline. **(03)**

Cut out the bodice templates

Cut along the lines through all the layers, and notch the Underbust position through all layers.

Separate the folded front bodice from the folded back bodice.

Working on the back template pieces placed with right sides together, mark 7.5cm (3 in) down the centre back from the top edge.

Draw a horizontal line from the 7.5-cm (3-in) mark. Cut away the portion above this line to establish the upper edge of the back bodice template. (04)

04

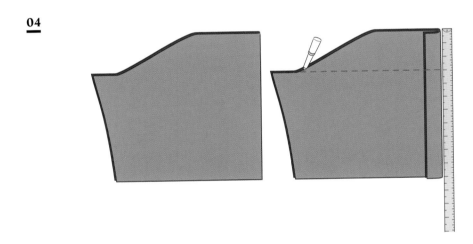

Lay the front bodice template over the back bodice template again. Fold down the length of the top at the half-Apex point.

Separate the front bodice template from the back bodice template. Invert all the dart creases that are protruding on the right side of the fabric.

With the dart lines on the fold, measure in 2cm (¾ in) from the front edge of the side panel at the Underbust and Waist.

Draw a line from the waistline that goes through both these marks and tapers to a point 16.5cm (6½ in) away, which is 6mm (¼ in) inch from the edge.

At the top edge corner, measure in 2.5cm (1 in). From here, draw a line that tapers to a point 7.5cm (3 in) away, which is 6mm (¼ in) from the edge. (05)

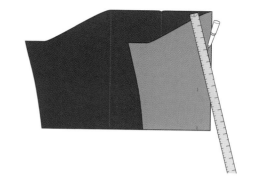

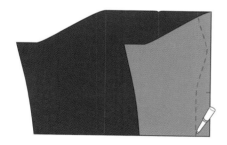

Join the points to create the dart seam/stitch line. (06)

Working on the back

With the dart lines folded, working to the left of the crease, measure in 2cm (¾ in) from the front edge of the side panel at the Underbust and Waist. Measure 6mm (¼ in) inwards along the top edge. (07)

Joint these points with straight lines to create the front edge of the side-back bodice panels.

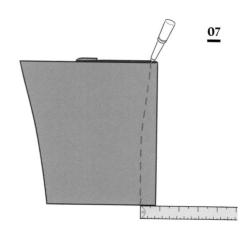

Pin and sew the front and back sections of the bodice together at the side seams, with a 2.5-cm (1-in) seam allowance. Test the fit, then once happy, move on to the next stage.

Centre front and centre back bodice panels

Cut along the centre-front fold. Cut away the zip allowance fold. (08)

Label the bodice panels

At the top of the centre-front panel, remove the excess and smooth out the style line. (09)

There are four panels. Label these as centre front (CF), side front (SF), side back (SB), and centre back (CB). If you are using striped fabric and want to create a chevron effect, draw a vertical line with an arrow at the top on each panel to show which way up it goes. Draw a line at 45° to the vertical line to establish the cross-grain. (**10**)

Cut all the seams along the sewn lines.

Be sure to notch the peak of the breast curve: this will help when putting the centre front and side front together. (**11**)

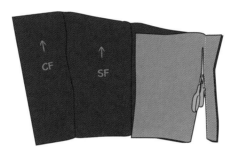

12

Cut panels of dress fabric

Next, use the templates for cutting out the bodice panels in dress material. Take the rest of the dress fabric and fold with right sides together. Pin the templates to the fabric with the cross-grain mark aligned with the straight grain of the fabric.

Working on the CF piece, extend the base by 12.5cm (5 in) to produce the wrapover section. At the tip of that line, draw a 5-cm (2-in) line upwards at a 90° angle.

From the top of the curved edge of the interlining, draw a diagonal line to the top of the 5-cm (2-in) line. (**12**)

Cut around the CF piece with a 1.2-cm (½-in) seam allowance (the piece now includes the extension).

Cut out the remaining bodice pieces

Cut around all the remaining pieces, adding a 1.2-cm (½-in) seam allowance.

Use these cut pieces of dress fabric as templates for cutting out lining and fusible interfacing pieces.

Belt

Cut out two pieces of dress fabric according to the measurements given in Pattern Pieces for strapless wrap dress.

Fold each piece in half along the length, with wrong sides together, and press.

Interfacing

Using an iron, affix the interfacing to the wrong side of all the lining pieces.

Join the bodice sections, dress and lining

With right sides together, match the CF piece to the SF piece along the curved edge and sew with a 1.2-cm (½-in) seam. Do this for both the dress and lining fabric.

Press the seams open.

Repeat for the CB and SB pieces.

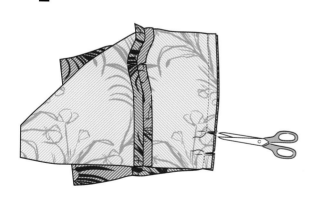

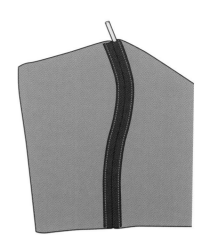

Boning channels

In the lining, sew down the pressed seam 1cm (³⁄₈ in) on either side of the CF/SF and CB/SB seamlines to create channels in which the plastic boning can be inserted. There is no boning on the SF/SB seamline. (13)

Belt hole

You will end up with one long piece for the dress fabric and one for the lining.

Create a belt hole in the right-hand side seam (as worn) of the bodice. Measuring up from the waistline, place a pin horizontally at 5.7cm (2¼ in) up the side seam. Place another at 4cm (1½ in) from the waistline.

Working on the dress fabric, snip the seam allowance to the sewn line at these points. Unpick the seam between these snips: this forms the belt hole. Secure the stitches above and below the belt hole by sewing a few stitches back and forth. (14)

Lay the lining over the dress fabric, wrong sides facing each other, so that you can determine the corresponding side seam in the lining. Repeat the step above to make a corresponding belt hole.

Bodice style line

Place the dress bodice and lining with right sides together and sew along the entire top seam (bodice style line) with a 1.2-cm (½-in) seam. Clip the seam and overstitch the seam to the lining. (15)

15

Sew the belt

Take the belt pieces, and fold each in half along the length with the right side inside. Do not press: you want the crease you made earlier to remain.

Sew along one short edge and the long edge with a 1.2-cm (½-in) seam. Clip the sewn corners.

Turn the belt right-side out through the unsewn short end. Press the sewn edges. Pleat along the open end to bring the width of it down to 5cm (2 in).

16

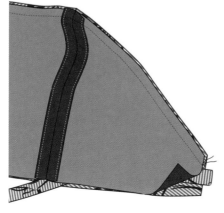

Attach the belt

Sandwich one belt between the lining and the dress fabric, so that the pleated end protrudes slightly from the tip of the extended CF bodice piece, adjacent to the waist seam and 1.2cm (½ in) above it. Sew with a 1.2-cm (½-in) seam. Repeat with the other belt on the opposite side. (16)

Finish the belt hole

17

Working on the inside of the garment, go back to the belt hole section and match the lining with the dress fabric, right sides facing. Sew the cut seam with a 1.2-cm (½-in) seam. (17)

Hem the skirt

Working on the skirt, hem the two straight front edges with a 1.2-cm (½-in) double-rolled hem (see page 15). Do the same with the hem.

Attach the skirt

Pin the waistline edge of the skirt fabric to the bodice, right sides together and keeping the lining clear so it doesn't get caught in the seam, and sew with a 1.2-cm (½-in) seam.

Boning

Insert the boning into the channels. I always tape around the ends of plastic boning first, to stop it bursting through the fabric.

Tuck the waistline seam in between the lining and dress fabric, fold the lining waist seam under by 1.2-cm (½-in), pin in place and do a catch stitch by hand. (18)

18

2nd date night dress

This timeless, fitted dress has a sweetheart bodice and lace upper bodice and sleeves. You can add optional embellishment to give it a romantic and truly bespoke feel. The design works equally well at different hem lengths: choose mini, knee-length or even a maxi length for an extra-special occasion. I personally prefer cotton lining because it gives me more hold and acts as a good body control and great foundation garment, but you will have your preference.

Measurements (see pages 19–23)

Horizontal
Back
Across Front
Across Back
Bust
Underbust
Waist
Hip

Vertical
Shoulder to Across Front
Shoulder to Across Back
Shoulder to Bust
Shoulder to Underbust

Shoulder to Waist
Shoulder to Hip
Shoulder to Hem

Other
Apex
Sweetheart bodice depth (SHD): measurement from your neck hollow to the desired depth of the centre-front bodice

Materials
Lace fabric, upper bodice and sleeves: 1m 37cm (1½ yd)
Dress fabric: see pattern pieces
Lining: polyester cotton, quantity as for dress

Matching thread
Zip: I always buy the longest length of zip because it's easy to shorten
Embellishments cut from spare lace fabric or store-bought.

Pattern pieces for romantic lace dress
Overall fabric dimensions for dress:
(Shoulder to hem) plus 4cm (1½ in) × Hip plus 35.5cm (14 in)

Equipment
Basic sewing project equipment

Method

Fold the fabric

Fold the dress fabric in half crossways (along the width; selvedges are at top and bottom) with the right side of the fabric inside. The folded edge forms the centre front of the dress. On the open side opposite the centre front fold, fold in 2.5cm (1 in) on both edges down the entire length, for the zip allowance at the centre back of the dress. Press these folds well. The top edge of the folded fabric piece will be the shoulder of the dress and the bottom edge will be the hem. At the centre back, make sure the raw edge and the folded zip allowance edge are aligned, then bring the centre-front fold over to align with the centre back. (**01**)

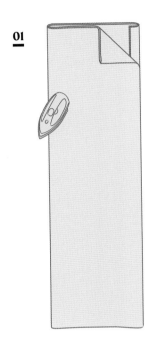

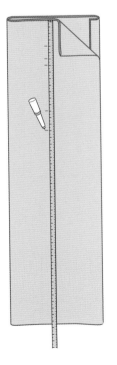

Place the vertical body measurements for front and back

On the new fold opposite the aligned centre front and centre back (the centre folds), measure down 18cm (7 in) from the top edge, to serve as the bustline.

Mark all the vertical body measurements plus 1.2cm (½ in) for a seam allowance, with two exceptions. Mark Shoulder to Across Front minus 2.5cm (1 in); and Shoulder to Across Back plus 2.5cm (1 in). Omit marking the Shoulder to Bust and Shoulder to Hem measurements. (**02**)

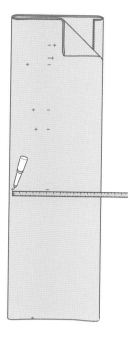

Place the horizontal body measurements for front and back

Now visualise these marked vertical measurements as straight lines running horizontally across the folded fabric. For example, the Shoulder to Waist mark will indicate the waistline. Each line will have a corresponding horizontal measurement that is measured along it to create the shape of the dress.

Divide the Across Front and Across Back measurements by two and add 1.2cm (½ in) to each. Mark each along the relevant Shoulder to Across Front and Shoulder to Across Back line (from the vertical body measurements), working from the centre folds and making a small cross.

Divide each of the remaining horizontal body measurements (Back, Bust, Underbust, Waist, Hips) by four and add 5cm (2 in). Mark these along the relevant horizontal line, working inwards from the centre folds, by making a small cross. For example, divide the Waist by four and add 5cm (2 in), marking this along the Shoulder to Waist horizontal line. Along the hem, replicate the measurement you worked out for the waistline. **(03)**

Create the side-seam shape

With a straight line, join the bustline cross to the waistline; from the hem, draw a straight line that stops 23cm (9 in) short of the cross at the hipline. From the waistline, draw a smooth curve that intercepts the hipline cross and merges with the top of the straight line coming up from the hem. **(04)**

Draw the neck

From the top corner of the centre folds, along the shoulder seam (top edge of the fabric), mark 9cm (3½ in) (mark 1) and your Back measurement divided by two, plus 1.2cm (½ in) (mark 2). Working from the same corner, measure and mark 9cm (3½ in) down the fold towards the hem (mark 3). Draw a concave curve between marks 1 and 3 to make the neckline. (05)

Create the armholes

From the cross at the bustline, draw a straight 5-cm (2-in) line towards the centre folds.

From mark 2 on the shoulder seam, draw a curved line that intercepts the cross at the Shoulder to Across Front and merges with the end of the 5-cm (2-in) line just drawn at the bustline. This is the front armhole.

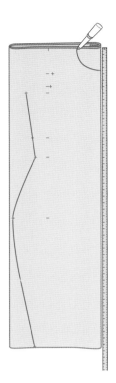

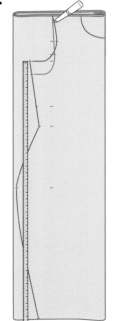

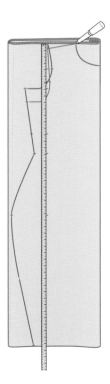

For the back armhole, measure downwards 5cm (2 in) from the cross at the bustline, and draw a straight line that runs parallel to the 5-cm (2-in) line above.

From mark 2 on the shoulder seam, draw a curve that intercepts the Across Back cross and merges with the parallel line just drawn. Make sure that the first 4cm (1½ in) of the curve, starting at the shoulder seam, merges with the front armhole. This completes the back armhole. (06)

To create the shoulder slope, measure and mark 2cm (¾ in) down from the top of the armholes; from here draw a line to the neck/shoulder point. This forms the shoulder seam. (07)

Cut out the front and back

You are now ready to cut. To start, cut around all the outer lines first, and do not cut away the different parts of the armhole. Make a small notch in the side seam, through all the layers, at Underbust, Waist and Hip level.

For the back armhole, lift the top layer off the bottom layer and redraw the back armhole on the bottom layer. Separate the front and back pieces of the dress, but keep the front folded in half, and keep the back pieces together. Cut out the front armhole and back armhole completely. (08)

08

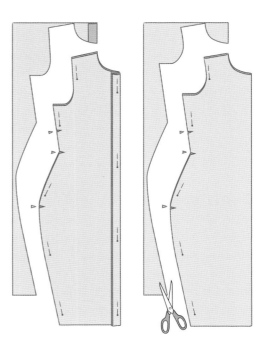

09

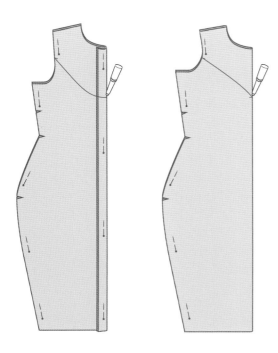

Sweetheart bodice

With the front of the dress still folded in half, place the tape measure level with the neck edge of the shoulder seam and mark the SHD minus 1.2cm (½ in).

With the front and back pieces of the dress together, from the top of the armhole at the shoulder, measure and mark 10cm (4 in).

Transfer these two markings to the back piece.

Working on the front piece, draw a curve that connects the mark at the armhole to the SHD, to create the sweetheart bodice shape.

Working on the back piece, draw a curve that flattens as it reaches the SHD on the back. (09)

Cut away these upper bodice pieces, having added a 1.2-cm (½-in) seam allowance above the lines of the sweetheart bodice. (10)

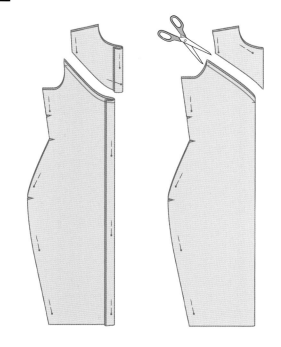

Lace upper bodice

Use the upper bodice pieces as templates to cut out the lace for the upper bodice area, adding a 2.5-cm (1-in) seam allowance where the lace will be attached to the sweetheart line of the dress. At the point of the sweetheart neckline, notch 1.2cm (½ in) up the fold. The picture shows the lace lying over the template piece, so that you know where the 2.5-cm (1-in) seam allowance is. Be sure to include the zip allowance in the lace back pieces also. (11)

Lining

Fold the lining fabric in half crossways (along the width), with the right side of the fabric inside and the selvedges top and bottom. On one open edge, fold over a 2.5-cm (1-in) zip allowance. Line up the centre-front dress piece against the fold of the lining and the centre-back dress piece against the zip allowance fold. Pin in place and cut exactly around the pieces, without adding any seam allowance.

Dart folds

Make the front bodice dart folds first. Working on the dress and lining front pieces (still pinned together), make a fold down the length of the front at the position of the Apex divided by two. Press to create a definite crease.

With the tape positioned vertically, make sure the 18cm (7 in) mark on the tape is level with the bustline (the base of the armhole), and then mark your Shoulder to Bust plus 1.2cm (½ in) along the pressed crease; this crease forms the centre line of the front darts and should be parallel with the centre folds.

Now make the bust dart folds. From the bustline, measure and mark 10cm (4 in) down the side seam. Press a crease from here to the line for the front darts you have just made, and don't exceed the mark on the first crease when pressing. This crease forms the centre line of the bust darts.

Snip a 1.2-cm (½-in) notch through the fold at the dip of the sweetheart bodice.

Invert all the dart creases that are projecting on the right side of the fabric in both dress fabric and lining: the dart creases need to project on the wrong side of the fabric. On the front piece, you should now have two sets of dart folds: the front dart folds and the bust dart folds. (12)

Shape the darts

Work on the front darts. Each dart is 1.2cm (½ in) wide at the Waist and Underbust. It tapers to a point 18cm (7 in) below the Waist, and 15cm (6 in) above the Waist. If the latter is beyond the bust point, end the dart 1.2cm (½ in) below the bust point.

Work on the bust darts. The dart is 2.5cm (1 in) wide at the side seam (outer edge). Measure 4cm (1½ in) along the fold from the outer edge. At this position the dart is still 2.5cm (1 in) deep; from here taper to a point 10cm (4 in) away on the fold.

Work on the back darts. Each dart is 1.2cm (½ in) wide at the Waist and Underbust. The dart tapers to a point 18cm (7 in) below the Waist and 23cm (9 in) above it.

Sew all the darts and press them, being careful not to press out the centre-front crease of the dress.

13

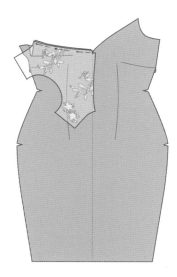

14

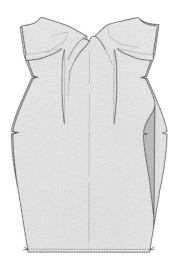

Attach the lace upper bodice

Working on the front piece of the lace upper bodice, match the notches you made at the point and dip of the sweetheart line of the dress piece, with the right sides facing each other. On one side, match up the rest of the seam, pin, and tack the lace in place; now match up the other side and tack. (**13**)

Along the same seams, line up the lining with the dress fabric (right sides facing each other), sandwiching the lace in between.

Tack in place, and then sew with a 1.2-cm (½-in) seam. Clip the seam and overstitch the seam to the lining. (**14**)

Flip the pieces over so that the right sides are facing each other and line up the hem, matching the centre-front creases. Sew along the hem with a 1.2-cm (½-in) seam, and understitch the seam to the lining. Press the seam. (**15**)

Work on the back upper bodice: as there are two back pieces, these steps will be done twice. Lay the lace on the dress fabric, with the right sides facing each other, and match up the centre-back creases. Pin in place.

Match up the seams at the armhole at the point where the distance from the seam to the armhole is 1.2cm (½ in). Pin in place.

Match up and pin the rest of the seam, easing the curves into each other. Tack.

Along the same seams, line up the lining with the dress fabric (right sides facing each other), sandwiching the lace in between. Tack and then sew with a 1.2-cm (½-in) seam. Clip the seam and overstitch the seam to the lining.

Flip the pieces over so that the right sides are facing each other and line up the hem, matching the zip allowance creases. Sew with a 1.2-cm (½-in) seam and overstitch the seam to the lining. Press the seam.

Back slit for ease of movement

Along the centre-back crease, mark your hipline and how high up from the hem you want the slit to reach. If the dress is a standard knee length, 18–20cm (7–8 in) is a good length for the slit.

Pin the two back pieces together at these marks and tack carefully along the zip allowance crease. Sew along the crease from 2.5cm (1 in) below the hipline to the second pin. Snip the zip allowance flap through all layers to this stitching line. Pull out the tacking thread. (16)

The next part has to be done one side at a time. At the hem area, pull the zip allowance flap on one side of the slit outwards so that the right side of the lining and the right side dress fabric are facing each other. Sew along the zip allowance crease to join the lining to the dress fabric along the slit. Clip the corners. Repeat on the other side of the slit.

Turn it right-side out and press.

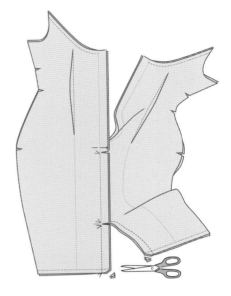

Side seams

Before sewing the side seams, pin the back pieces together along the zip allowance fold.

Lay the front piece over the back piece, right sides together, making sure the front centre crease and the zip allowance are lined up, and the side seam notches are sitting at the same level.

With one hand holding down the pieces at centre-waist level, gently pull the lining out of the way and then grip the right side seams with one finger in between the layers; be sure not to involve the back lining. Pull both layers taut and pin flat, with the pin about 4cm (1½ in) inside the edge. You may find that the seams don't match up perfectly, but this is fine. Repeat for the other side, and then again for both sides at Underbust and Hip levels. At the bustline and hemline, match up the sides perfectly and pin.

Now take the Bust, Underbust, Waist and Hip measurements, divide them by four and mark these along the relevant levels as before, marking from the centre crease outwards only on the right-hand side. (17)

Join up the marks up as previously. Flip the garment around so that the back is on top and using the tape measure, copy the seam allowance to the other side seam. Sew along the lines made.

Turn the garment so that the lining has its right sides facing each other, inside. Repeat the side-seam process.

Sew the lace shoulder seams with a 1.2-cm (½-in) seam, and then sew a parallel row 3mm (1/8 in) above that. Carefully snip off the seam close to the stitching. (18)

Check the fit of the dress and make any necessary adjustments.

Zip

Insert a zip (see page 18).

Hem
Hem the bottom edge with a double-turned hem.

Sleeves

Cut out a fitted sleeve in lace fabric (see pages 24–26). Sew the seam of the sleeve with a double row of stitching, as for the shoulder seam, and cut away the excess. Do the same with the armhole seam after attaching the sleeve to the dress.

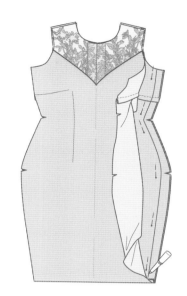

Optional embellishment

Arrange the embellishment around the neckline or chosen location, and use stab stitch around each piece to secure in place.

Showstopping maxi

Everyone needs a glamorous piece of occasion wear. Social media, Instagram and Facebook have helped to make the world so much smaller: now multicultural influences abound and conservative evening looks have been swapped for more adventurous shapes, fabrics and textures. This strappy dress with a crossover bodice is a classic shape realised in a beautiful duchesse satin; I played with texture and added bejewelled three-dimensional lace embellishments in contrasting black. I chose duchesse satin because it has just enough structure to give the skirt the voluptuous fall I desire without being too 'sticky-outy'. The design can be made in a softer fabric, such as a floral crêpe de Chine (perfect for a spring wedding), or chiffon (if you're feeling brave as it's harder to handle!).

Measurements (see pages 19–23)

Horizontal
Back
Across Front
Across Back
Bust
Underbust
Waist
Hips

Vertical
Shoulder to Across Front
Shoulder to Across Back
Shoulder to Bust
Shoulder to Underbust
Shoulder to Waist
Shoulder to hem

Other
Apex
Front neckline depth: neck hollow to desired depth
Back neckline depth: nape of neck to desired depth

Pattern pieces for showstopping maxi

Flared skirt formula: waist measurement divided by 3.14 = first radius
First radius plus (Shoulder to waist pus 38cm/1½ in) = second radius

Materials
Dress fabric: 4.5m (5 yd) × 150cm (60 in) wide

Lining for bodice: Bust plus 45cm (½ yd) × 115cm (45 in) wide
Lining for skirt: 2nd radius × 2 × 115cm (45 in) wide (knee-length lining), or 150cm (60 in) wide (full-length lining)
Matching thread
Strong thread for turning straps
Interfacing (lightweight or medium-weight): Bust plus 45cm (½ yd) × 115cm (45 in) wide
Embellishment (optional)
Zip: use the longest length as you can always cut it down

Equipment
Basic sewing project equipment
Fat hand-sewing needle for turning the straps

Method

Prepare the skirt fabric

Fold the skirt fabric across the width (so the selvedges are top and bottom) with right sides together and then fold over on the bias (this fold will be the centre front of the garment), by bringing the edge over to lie 2.5cm (1 in) from the open edge opposite (this is the centre back). In the final dress, the hem curves down and is longer at the back than the front.

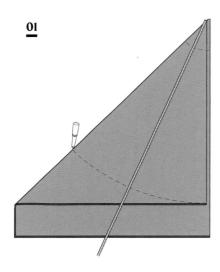

01

Cut out the skirt

Using the tape measure as a 'compass', place one end at the top corner of the folded fabric, and pivot it to mark the first and second radius (see Pattern Pieces). Draw marks at regular intervals and join to form a smooth curve. The curve formed by the second radius is the front hemline. (01)

Next, draw a curve for the back hemline. Measuring from the front hemline, place marks 20cm (8 in) below it at regular intervals. (02)

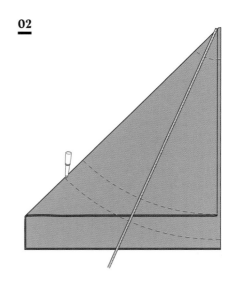

02

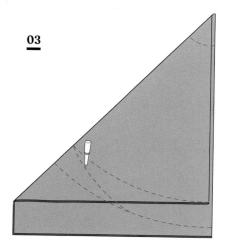

03

From the diagonal fold and starting at the front hemline, draw a smooth curve that lands halfway along the back hemline. (03)

04

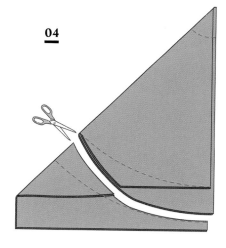

Cut along the back hemline following this connecting curve to the folded edge. (04)

05

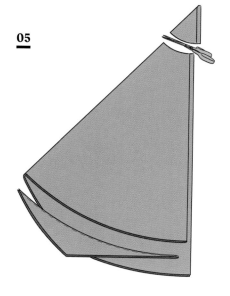

Now, cut completely along the front hemline, but only through the top two layers of fabric, then cut the first radius plus a 1.2-cm (½-in) seam allowance. Measure 23cm (9 in) down the centre-back seam and place a notch. (05)

Skirt lining

If you want the skirt to be fully lined, repeat the skirt steps to make a lining. However, I have made the skirt lining shorter than the dress fabric, because I don't want it lined all the way and it is more economical on fabric. The bodice is fully lined.

Bodice

To create the bodice, you will first work with the lining fabric, then use these pieces as a template to cut the dress fabric.

Fold the bodice lining fabric in half lengthways, with right sides together. This fold will be the centre front of the garment. On both open edges opposite, fold over a 2.5-cm (1-in) zip allowance towards the centre front. Press. The zip allowance edge is the centre back.

Bring the centre front over to align with the centre back. The top edge forms the shoulder seam edge and the bottom edge forms the waistline seam.

06

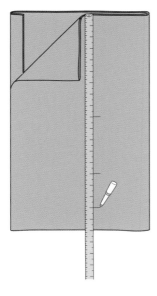

Bodice construction

The front bodice consists of a crossover, bra-like upper section with thin straps, which is joined to an underbust band. The back is the same shape. The underbust band is sewn to the skirt.

Place the vertical body measurements

Measure down from the shoulder seam and place marks as follows: at 23cm (9 in), at Shoulder to Underbust plus 1.2cm (½ in), and at Shoulder to Waist plus 1.2cm (½ in). Visualise these marks as horizontal lines: the first one is the bustline, the second is the underbust line, and the third is the waistline. (06)

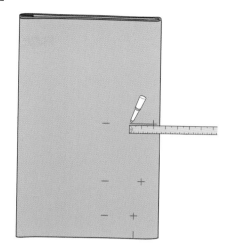

Place the horizontal body measurements

At the vertical reference points you have just made, mark the corresponding horizontal measurements for the Bust, Underbust and Waist with a small cross as follows: (each measurement divided by four) plus 5cm (2 in). At the bottom edge of the bodice, mark as follows: (Waist divided by four) plus 5cm (2 in). From the cross at the bustline, draw a straight 5-cm (2-in) line back towards the centre folds (07).

Side and shoulder seams

Join all the crosses for the side with straight lines. Measuring along the shoulder seam edge from the centre folds, place two marks as follows: at 7.5cm (3 in), and your Back divided by two. At about halfway between the shoulder seam edge and the bustline, measuring from the centre folds, mark a cross as follows: Across Front divided by two. (08)

From the second mark along the shoulder seam, draw an armhole curve that intercepts the Across Front cross and joins the end of the 5-cm (2-in) line at the bustline. Draw a horizontal line across the bodice 7.5cm (3 in) above the waistline edge. (09)

Measure 2cm (¾ in) vertically downwards from the top of the armhole along the shoulder seam edge. From that point, draw a diagonal line that hits the inner shoulder seam. This completes the shoulder slope. (The cut-away shape will be created later.)

08

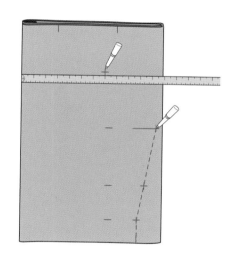

09

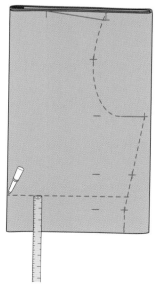

Cut out along the lines through all the layers, including the line drawn 7.5cm (3 in) above the hem. Set this bottom panel aside: it is the lining for the band under the bust. (**10**)

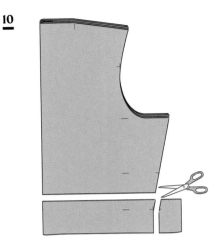

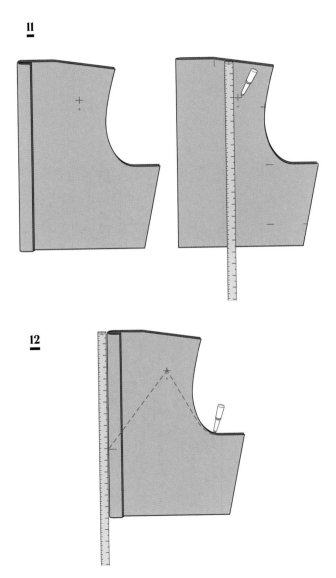

Refine the bodice shape

Working on the front and back bodice pieces, measure and mark 5cm (2 in) inside the Across Front mark towards the centre front or centre back. From the shoulder seam, in line with the mark just made, measure downwards and place a small cross at 7.5cm (3 in). (**11**)

Working on the back piece, decide how low you want the upper edge of the back bodice to be at the centre back. Mark this on the centre-back seam, measuring down from the top edge. From this centre-back mark, draw a diagonal line to the small cross. From the cross, draw a line that slightly curves as it lands at the deepest section of the armhole curve. (**12**)

Cut along these lines and set the back pieces aside.

Refine the front bodice shape

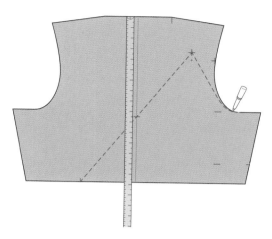

The front bodice pieces lap over each other. The following instructions will create one piece; use this piece as a template to create the opposite side.

Unfold the front bodice piece. Measuring from the top edge, mark the front neckline depth along the centre-front crease. From the cross 5cm (2 in) inside the Across Front mark, draw a diagonal line to the waist that intercepts the front neckline depth mark. Again from the cross, draw a line that slightly curves as it lands at the deepest section of the armhole curve. (13)

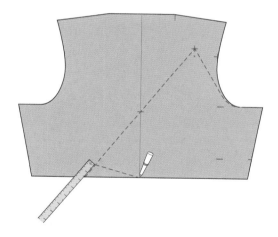

From the waistline, measure and mark 5cm (2 in) along the diagonal line. From that point, draw a curve that lands at the bottom of the centre front. (14)

Place a small cross for the Shoulder to Bust mark by measuring down from the highest part of the shoulder seam.

Dress fabric

Cut out the shaped lining pieces and use them as templates to cut out identical dress fabric pieces. Notch the centre-front crease at the waistline through all pieces.

Darts

With the lining and dress fabric pieces still together, line up the centre back behind the centre-front crease. Measuring from the centre-front crease, fold and press a vertical crease through all the pieces at your half-Apex point (Apex divided by two). These form the dart creases. (**15**)

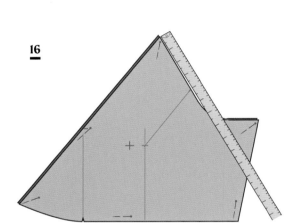

16

Working on the front, transfer the Shoulder to Bust cross to the dart crease. Measure 10cm (4 in) down the armhole and mark. Press a crease that connects these two marks. The point where the creases meet is the bust point. (**16**)

Invert all creases so that they project on the wrong side of the fabric.

Working on the front pieces, the front darts are 1.2cm (½ in) wide at the underbust band seam and Underbust, then taper to a point 1.2cm (½ in) below the bust point.

At the armhole, the dart is 2.5cm (1 in) wide at the outer edge. It tapers to a point 7.5cm (3 in) along the crease and 6mm (¼ in) away from edge of the crease.

Working on the back pieces, the dart is 1.2cm (½ in) wide at the underbust band seam and Underbust, then tapers to a point 20cm (8 in) away.

Sew all the darts.

Straps

To make the straps, cut a square scrap of fabric.
Line up one of the edges against the adjacent edge
to create a bias fold (right sides together). Press.

Make a strip that is 3cm (1¼ in) wide by placing
marks at this distance from the fold at close
intervals. Cut along this line, then cut through the
fold to give two bias strips.

Fold each strip in half with the right side inside.
Sew down the entire length 1cm (⅜ in) from the
fold. Trim the seam to 6mm (¼ in).

Double-thread a needle with strong thread. Loop
the thread around the top of the strip and tie it
very tightly. Slip the eye end of the needle down
inside the strip and feed it through to the other end.
Gently pull on the needle until the end of the strip
enters the tube. Continue gently pulling until the
strap is completely turned out. (**17**)

Cut the length of the strips down to 20cm (8 in).
Press each strap so that the seam lies centrally
(this allows it to lie against the body and
remain unseen).

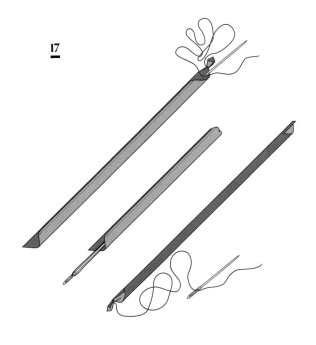

17

Band

Working on the folded underbust band pieces, cut
off 2.5cm (1 in) from the end, through all layers.
Use this as a template to cut out identical pieces of
dress fabric and interfacing. Apply the interfacing
to the band.

Attach the front bodice lining

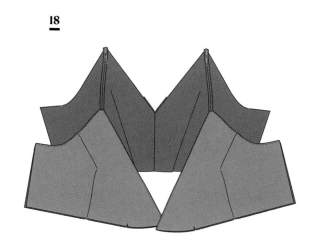

Working on the right side of the dress fabric front piece, pin the strap to the top of the bra shape; make sure the seamline of the strap faces upwards. Lay the lining over the dress fabric, right sides together and with the strap sandwiched in between. Sew along the neckline and armhole edge with a 1.2-cm (½-in) seam. Clip the point and clip the armhole curve. (**18**)

Understitch the seams to the lining to keep them from rolling into view. Press.

19

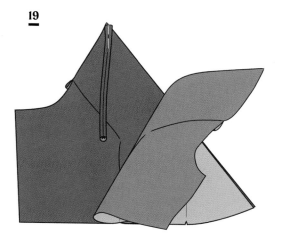

Attach the back bodice lining

Pin the other end of the strap to the back dress fabric pieces, as pictured. Adjust the length of the strap if necessary. Open the zip allowance flaps, lay the lining over the dress fabric, right sides together, and then sew along the neckline and armhole with a 1.2-cm (½-in) seam. Clip the point, the armhole, and the dip at the top of the zip allowance crease. (19)

Cut off the protruding seam at the top of the zip allowance flap.

Complete the bodice sections

Overlap the front pieces at the waist notch and pin together along the centre-front crease. Repeat for the two back pieces, pinning together along the zip allowance crease. Lay the front over the back, right sides facing. Push the lining out of the way and pin the side seams of the back and front dress fabric together. From the centre front, measure and mark along the bustline towards the side as follows: Bust divided by four. Do the same for the Underbust along the underbust band seam. Join up the marks with straight lines: this is the seam allowance. Copy the seam allowance to the other side. Sew along the line, then repeat for the lining, making sure the lining is right sides together. (20)

Remove all pins and test the fit.

20

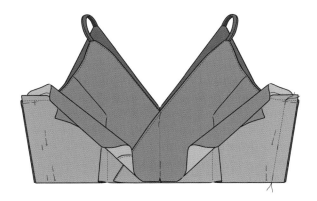

Attach bra shape to underbust band

Take the lined bra shape and the band, place with right sides together and matching the lower edge of the bra with the upper edge of the band. Repeat with the band lining. Make sure the centre front and centre back align in each case. Sew with a 1.2-cm (½-in) seam. The bra will be sandwiched between the underbust band and its lining. (21)

21

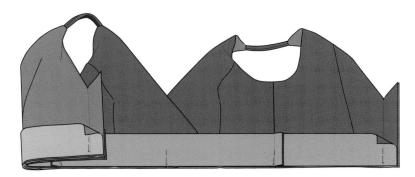

Sew underbust band to skirt

Working with the dress fabric, match the lower edge of the band to the top of the skirt, right sides together and with the centre front aligned. Sew with a 1.2-cm (½-in) seam. Repeat with the lining.

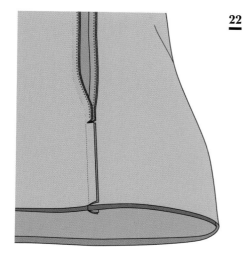

22

Insert the zip

With right sides together, sew the centre-back seam of the skirt from the 23cm (9 in) mark to the hem with a 2.5-cm (1-in) seam. Repeat with the lining.

At the 23-cm (9-in) point, snip the seam to the stitching line for both lining and dress fabric.

Place the wrong side of the unsewn zip allowance fold of the lining against the wrong side of the dress fabric; the snips you made earlier will help you do this. Zigzag the raw edges of each side together, and you will then work with them as one piece. (If you find it helpful, you may sew the lining and dress fabric together along the zip allowance fold: it enables you to work with them as a single piece.) **(22)**

Insert the zip (see page 16).

Hem

Hem the bottom edge of both the dress and the lining with a double-turned hem.

Embellishments

If you are applying embellishments, pin in place and once you're happy with the position, carefully hand-sew them to the dress.

Child's peekaboo-back dress

L ittle girls' dresses are always a pleasure to make, even more so now that I have a little girl of my own. The great thing about sewing for a pre-pubescent girl is that because she doesn't yet have curves, complex garment construction and darting are not required and clothes can be made of simple shapes. So if you're a sewing newbie, little girls' dresses can be a good place to start your dressmaking journey. Try making this dress in a novelty-print cotton for a fun summer look; you can omit a lining and bias-bind the raw edges instead. The version shown here is a more formal look, using beautiful gunmetal grey duchesse satin.

Measurements (see pages 19–23)

Horizontal
Back
Chest
Waist

Vertical
Shoulder to Waist
Shoulder to hem

Other
Arm Scye: loop the tape measure around the top of the shoulder and under the armpit. Don't hold the tape too tightly

Pattern pieces for child's peekaboo-back dress
Bodice fabric:
Largest horizontal measurement plus 25.5cm (10 in) × (Shoulder to Waist) plus 2.5cm (1 in)
Full-circle skirt formula:
(Waist divided by 3.14) divided by 2 = first radius
First radius plus skirt length plus 2.5cm (1 in) = second radius
Skirt fabric:
(Second radius × 2) + 5cm (2 in) × (second radius × 2) + 5cm (2 in)

Materials
Dress fabric: a maximum of 2.75m (3 yd) × 115cm (45 in) or 150cm (60 in) wide
Lining: as for dress fabric
Matching thread
Zip
Appliqué (optional)
Hook and eye

Equipment
Basic sewing project equipment

Method

Fold and cut the skirt fabric

Fold the fabric in half with the right side inside, and press the fold (this will be the centre front of the skirt). On one open edge, fold in a 2.5-cm (1-in) zip allowance. At the centre back, make sure the raw edge and the folded zip allowance edge are aligned, then bring the centre-front fold over to align with the centre back. These are the centre folds.

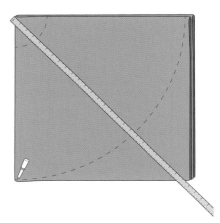

From the top corner of the centre folds, and using the tape as a 'compass', pivot and mark the first radius and second radius with a smooth curve. (01)

You now have two quarter-circles, one for the front of the skirt and one for the back. Working on the piece with the zip allowance fold, cut through the fold opposite the zip allowance. Use these pieces as templates to cut out identical lining pieces in the same manner. Set the skirt pieces aside.

Folding and cut the bodice fabric

Fold the fabric in half crossways with the right side of the fabric inside. This will be the centre front of the bodice. On the open edges opposite, fold in a 2.5-cm (1-in) zip allowance (folding both layers of fabric together) for the centre back of the bodice.

Bring the centre-front fold over to align with the centre back. These are the centre folds. The top edge of the folded fabric piece will be the shoulder of the bodice and the bottom edge will be the waist edge.

Place the vertical body measurements for front and back

Place the head of the tape level with the shoulder seam and mark the chest line as follows: (Arm Scye divided by two) minus 1.2cm (½ in).

Measuring from the centre folds outwards, mark a point along the chest line with a small cross as follows: (Bust divided by four) plus 2.5cm (1 in). Then mark a point along the waist edge with a small cross as follows: (Waist divided by four) plus 2.5cm (1 in).

From the cross at the chest line, draw a 2.5-cm (1-in) horizontal line towards the centre folds.

Join the crosses with a straight line. (02)

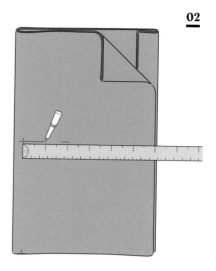

02

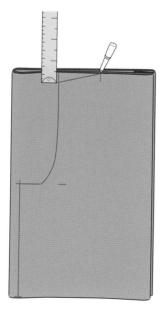

03

Create the armhole and neckline

Along the shoulder seam and measuring from the centre folds, mark as follows: (Back divided by two) plus 1.2cm (½ in). Mark 5cm (2 in) from that point towards the centre.

Draw a curved line that joins the first mark along the shoulder to the end of the 2.5-cm (1-in) line at the chest line. This forms the armhole.

At the top of the armhole, measure 1.2cm (½ in) downward and draw a sloping line that connects to the top of the neck edge of the shoulder seam. (03)

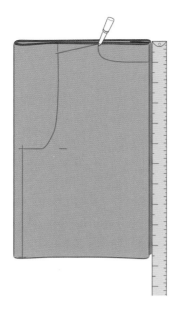

04

Measure 4cm (1½ in) down the centre folds and draw a curved neckline that connects to the inner shoulder point. (04)

Cut out the front and back bodice

Cut around the markings and separate the front from the back.

Lining

Prepare pieces for the dress lining as for the skirt and bodice.

05

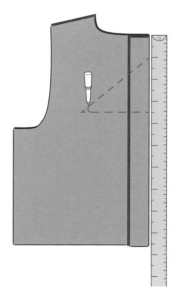

Back bodice

Create the 'peekaboo' cut-out on the back bodice: measuring along the centre back, place a mark at 2.5cm (1 in) and 9cm (3½ in).

Working horizontally from the 9-cm (3½-in) mark, draw a straight 7.5-cm (3-in) line. Connect the end of the line to the 2.5-cm (1-in) mark. This will produce a half-triangle shape. Soften the base corner of the triangle with a curve. Cut along the lines. Repeat on the back bodice lining pieces. (05)

Front of dress

Attach the skirt to the bodice. Join the waistlines of the skirt and bodice, matching the centre fronts, and pin along the seam. Start from the centre and work your way outwards. You may find that the skirt is slightly bigger than the bodice at the waistline, but you can correct this as you sew the side seams. Repeat with the lining pieces. (06)

06

Work on the front bodice. Place the lining and the dress fabric with right sides together, matching them up along the neckline.

Sew along the neckline with a 1.2-cm (½-in) seam allowance, then clip the seam and understich the seam allowance to the lining. With right sides together, match up the hems of the lining and skirt. Sew with a 1.2-cm (½-in) seam, then clip the seam. (07)

Understitch the seam allowance to the lining and press all the seams.

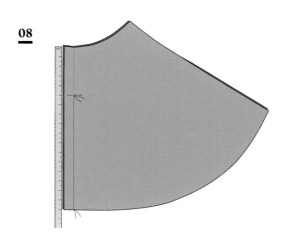

07

08

Back skirt

Place the back skirt pieces with right sides together. Measuring down from the waist at the centre back, place a pin at 12.5cm (5 in) along the zip allowance crease. (08)

Sew the two back skirt pieces together below the pin, along the crease towards the hem. Repeat for the lining.

Back bodice

Work on the back bodice and lining. Place the lining over the dress fabric, right sides together, with the zip allowance unfolded. Sew along the crease, from the neck to the next edge (top of cut-out section).

Sew the neckline from the shoulder to the back neck with a 1.2-cm (½-in) seam. Clip the seam, and understitch the seam to the lining for as far as you can. (09)

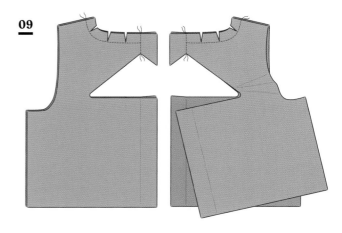

09

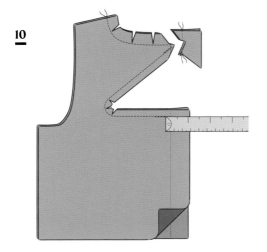

10

Sew around the cut-out section with a 1-cm (³/₈-in) seam. Stop 1.2cm (½ in) before reaching the zip allowance crease at centre back. Clip the seam and understitch the seam to the lining as far as possible. (10)

Child's Peekaboo-back Dress

Attach back skirt

With the zip folds open, match the centre back of the skirt to the centre back of the bodice at the waistline. Start pinning from the central crease, as with the front. Sew with a 1.2-cm (½-in) seam. Repeat for the lining.

With right sides together, match up the hems of the lining and skirt. Sew with a 1.2-cm (½-in) seam, then clip the seam.

Armholes

On the armholes of each piece, turn the lining and fabric so that they are right sides facing.

Sew along the armhole with a 1.2-cm (½-in) seam. Clip the seam and overstitch the fabric to the lining. Press all the armholes. (11)

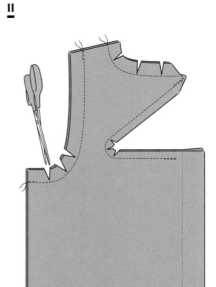

11

12

Side seams

Lay the front piece over the back with the right sides facing. Push the lining out of the way and match the chest and waistline seams, pinning them together. Sew the side seam from armhole to waistline with a 1.2-cm (½-in) seam. (12)

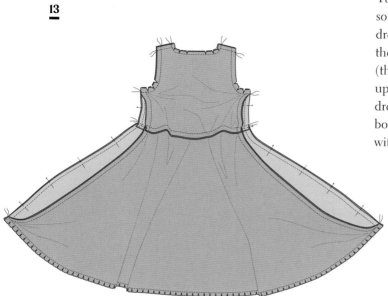

13

Turn the dress completely inside out so that the right sides of the lining and dress are facing each other. Match up the waistline seams of fabric and lining (the chest line will already be matched up as it was sewn when sewing the dress fabric side seams). Sew from the bottom of the armhole to the hem with a 1.2-cm (½-in) seam. **(13)**

Shoulder seams

Turn the dress right side out through the centre back opening. Overlock or use zigzag stitch to join the fabric and lining together at the shoulder. With the fabric right sides together, sew the shoulder seam with a 1.2-cm (½-in) seam. Press the seam open.

Zip

Insert the zip (see page 16). Hand-sew a hook and eye attachment to the back neckline.

Embellishment

Try trimming the waist with fancy ribbon to finish the dress. I used some beautiful three-dimensional lace appliqué in a contrasting colour, stitched on by hand, for extra wow factor!

Button-back shirt dress

T his is a fun twist on a classic shirt, literally. I have taken a man's shirt, twisted it around so it buttons down the back, and resized it to hug a woman's curves better. It makes a simple, yet very effective shirt dress that has a freshness to it. The man's shirt forms the upper part of the dress and a striking flounce, which skims the knee, forms the lower part. I have chosen a bold, graphic design to complement the plain shirt.

Measurements
(see pages 19–23)

Horizontal
Back
Bust
Underbust
Waist
Hips

Vertical
Shoulder to Bust
Shoulder to Underbust
Shoulder to Waist
Shoulder to Hips
Shoulder to Hem

Pattern pieces for button-back shirt dress
Flounce formula:
[(Length of the curve from base of front dart to hemline × 2) plus the shirt hem's measurement] divided by 6.28, and rounded up to the nearest half or whole number = first radius
(Extra length required for dress plus first radius) plus 4cm (1½ in) = second radius
Flounce material:
(Second radius × two) × (second radius × two)

Materials
Man's cotton shirt, buttoning all the way down the front, in a very large size (chest size in and above; any length)
Contrasting cotton fabric: 3m (3¼ yd) × 115cm (45 in) wide
Matching thread

Equipment
Basic sewing project equipment

Method

01

Prepare the man's shirt

Carefully cut off the sleeves along the join to the body of the shirt.

Straighten the base of the shirt by cutting straight across to remove the curved hem. (01)

Make sure the shirt is lying perfectly flat, and pin it down the middle of the button placket for the length of the shirt, through the front and back layers.

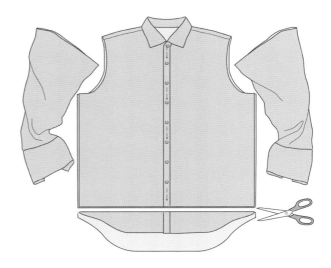

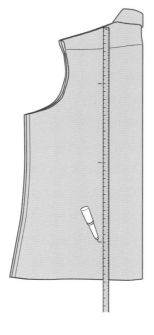

02

Place the vertical body measurements for front and back

Fold the shirt in half. Place the head of the tape measure at the highest part of the shoulder seam, and measure down to make three marks: at 18cm (7 in), the Shoulder to Waist measurement, and Shoulder to hip. The first mark is the bustline, the second the waistline, and the last the hipline. (02)

Place the horizontal measurements for front and back

Along the bustline, measure and mark with a small cross as follows: (Bust divided by four) plus 5cm (2 in). Do the same along the waistline and hipline, using the same formula with the Waist and hip measurements.

From the folded edge of the shirt, measure and mark along the shoulder seam as follows: (Back divided by four) plus 1.2cm (½ in). **(03)**

03

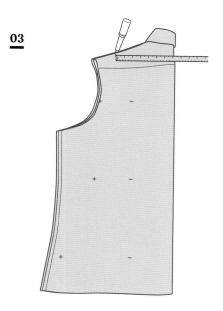

04

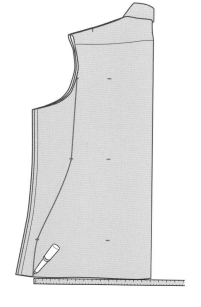

Side seams

Join the first two crosses at the side of the garment with a straight line, then extend the line to the cross at the hipline, slightly rounding it out as you do so.

Along the straightened bottom edge of the shirt, put a cross at the same distance from the centre as on the hipline.

Join the crosses with a straight line. **(04)**

Armholes

From the cross at the bustline, draw a 2.5-cm (1-in) straight line in towards the centre of the garment.

Draw an armhole curve that begins from the mark at the shoulder and ends at the end of the 2.5-cm (1-in) line. **(05)**

Cut along the lines; the shoulder seams will keep the shirt attached. The front of the original shirt will now become the back of the dress.

05

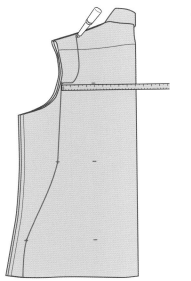

06

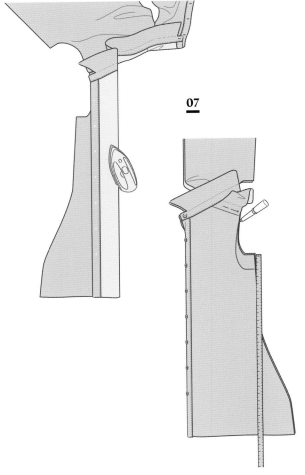

07

Dress back

Work on the back of the dress (the buttoned part). Divide the Apex by two, measure this distance from the button placket, and fold along the length of the shirt at this point. Press. **(06)**

For the back dart, measure 1.2cm (½ in) out from the fold at the waist and make a mark. From this mark draw a slanting line upwards that measures 23cm (9 in) and finishes at the folded edge. From the same waist mark draw a slanting line downwards that measures 18cm (7 in) and finishes at the folded edge. Repeat on the other half of the back.

From the base of the armhole, measure and mark 5cm (2 in) down the side seam.

Copy the above armhole curve at that point to the other back armhole area and cut out. **(07)**

Dress front

Work on the front of the dress. Place the back pieces over the front and copy the back darts onto the wrong side of the front for the front darts. For the side bust darts, measure 10cm (4 in) down the side seam from the bottom of each armhole and make a mark (A). From the highest point of the shoulder seam, mark the Shoulder to Bust measurement along the fold line (B) of each front dart. Fold and press a crease from A to B. From A, measure 2.5cm (1 in) towards the armhole along the side edge. Measure 4cm (1½ in) from the side edge along the A/B fold. Join the two new marks or the side bust darts on each side of the front.

Sew all the darts for front and back. Press.

Place the front and back of the dress with right sides together and sew the side seams with a 1.2-cm (½-in) seam.

Sleeves

To resize the man's shirt sleeves, lay the sleeves on top of each other and follow the instructions for sleeves (see page 24). The existing sleeve head (where the sleeve fits into the armhole) will serve as a good guide for drawing the curves of the sleeve head.

Sew the sleeve seams with a 1.2-cm (½-in) seam. Turn up a double hem.

08

Insert the sleeves

Turn the sleeves right side out and the dress inside out. With right sides together, put the sleeve head into the armhole. Pin in place, matching the side seams and the centre sleeve-head notch with the shoulder seam. (08)

Sew in place with a 1.2-cm (½-in) seam. (Note that in a classic man's shirt, the shoulder is not indicated by a seam because of the yoke; however, it always has a crease at the shoulder, so that is what you will match the sleeve-head notch with.)

Cut out the flounce

Measure the entire hem of the dress.

From the base of one of the front darts, draw a curve to about halfway along the front hem in the direction of the opposite side seam. This curve must not land on the hem at too sharp an angle. **(09)**

Cut a square piece of the contrasting fabric (see formulae in Pattern Pieces). Fold it in half with the right sides together, and in half again along the other edge.

10

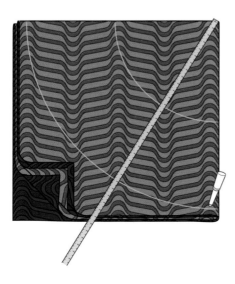

Place the tape measure at the corner that only has folded edges and no open edges, then use it as a 'compass' and pivot to mark the first and second radiuses. Cut along the lines. **(10)**

Unfold once and cut open along one of the folds.

Attach the flounce

Hem the bottom edge of the flounce and its short ends with a narrow, double-turned hem (see page 15).

With right sides together, sew the inner edge of the flounce to the hem of the dress, starting at the top of the curved line and working around the hem. There will be an overlap at the hem. Topstitch the frill to the dress along the curve.

<u>11</u>

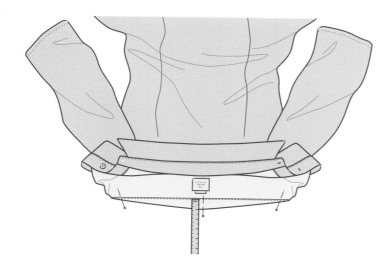

Yoke seam dart

You need to create a dart in the yoke seam at the front of the dress, to improve the fit in the front neck area (because it was originally cut for the back). The lining of the yoke in a man's shirt is usually made in two pieces, so the centre seam of this indicates the exact middle of the yoke.

At this middle point, pinch a 2.5-cm (1-in) dart that tapers to a point just before the armhole on each side. Pin in place, and then sew in the yoke seam. Press the dart down. (11)

Child's shirt dress

T his type of project is what comes to mind when I think of
upcycling: taking an old garment and giving it a whole new life
– a new purpose and the opportunity for a new story. Aside from the
sustainability factor, the sentimental value that can be added warms
my heart; this is one of my husband's old shirts that I have transformed
into a dress for our daughter. Give it a go! You need quite a large
shirt, because there are quite a few pieces in this design. If you are
making the dress for a bigger child, and have difficulty getting a very
large shirt, use some contrasting fabric to make up the shortfall. I have
made this dress to match the adult's Button-Back Shirt Dress (see page
130), although the child's version buttons up the front.

Measurements
(see pages 19–23)

Horizontal
Back
Chest
Waist

Vertical
Shoulder to Waist
Shoulder to hem

Other
Arm Scye (armhole: take this
measurement by looping the
tape measure around the top
of the shoulder and under the
armpit. Don't hold the tape
too tightly)

Materials
Small man's cotton shirt,
buttoned down its full length
Contrasting fabric: 1m (1 yd) ×
150cm (45 in) wide (optional)
Lightweight fusible interfacing:
50cm (20 in) wide
Matching thread

Pattern pieces for baby's dress
Sleeve formulae:
Arm Scye divided by 3.14,
rounded to the nearest whole or
half number = first radius
First radius plus 5cm (2 in) =
second radius

Equipment
Basic sewing project equipment

Method

Prepare the shirt

Lay the shirt flat, with the front facing upwards. Carefully cut away the sleeves and across the upper chest, just beneath the collar. Set these pieces aside. Cut along the side seams too. (01)

01

02

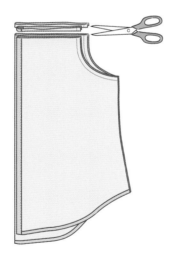

Fold the front shirt in half, with right sides together. Do the same for the back shirt. Lay the front piece on the back piece, making sure the side seams are lined up.

Level off the top edge to make sure that all the edges align. This will give you a nice straight edge to work from. (02)

Place the vertical measurements for the bodice

Place the head of the tape measure at the top edge, and measure and mark downwards to place the Chest mark as follows: (Arm Scye divided by two) plus 1.2cm (½ in).

03

Place a mark as follows: Shoulder to Waist plus 2.5cm (1 in). Draw a horizontal line. Cut along this line, through all the layers. This is going to become the bodice; set it aside. **(03)**

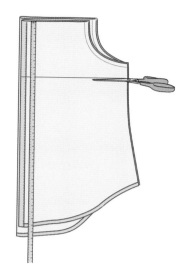

Place the vertical measurements for the skirt

Measuring upwards from the lowest point of the shirt's original hem, place a mark as follows: (Shoulder to hem minus Shoulder to Waist) plus 1.2cm (½ in).

Draw a horizontal line along this marking and cut through all layers. **(04)**

Draw another horizontal line along the bottom of the shirt to get rid of the curved hem. Discard the curved bottom section. The top section will be shaped into the bodice, the middle section will be box pleated for the skirt and the narrow bottom section is the pattern for the contrast strip. **(05)**

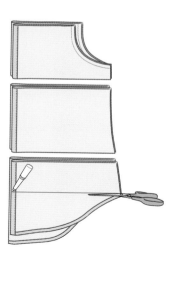

Place the horizontal measurements for the bodice

With the folded front and back pieces on top of each other, as before, work on the bodice again. From the centre folds, measure outwards along the top edge (this is the shoulder edge) and place a mark as follows: (Back divided by two) plus 1.2cm (½ in).

Along the Chest line, working from the centre folds outwards, measure and mark a cross as follows: (Chest divided by four) plus 2.5cm (1 in). Repeat this formula with the Waist measurement and mark this along the bottom edge. (06)

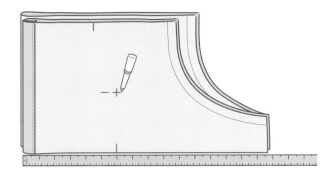

06

Draft the shoulder and armhole

Connect the mark at the shoulder edge to the cross at the Chest line with a curve, to form the armhole.

Then connect the Chest-line cross with the mark you made along the Waist hem, using a straight line.

From the marking at the top edge, measure and mark 7.5cm (3 in) towards the centre folds. This will create the neckline edge of the shoulder seam. (07)

Shape the neckline

From the top edge, measure down the centre folds and place a mark at 2.5cm (1 in).

Draw a curve that connects this with the neckline edge of the shoulder seam. This forms the neckline.

Shape the shoulder

From the outer marking on the shoulder edge, measure 1.2cm (½ in) down the armhole curve. From there, draw a diagonal line to connect to the neckline of the shoulder seam. Cut along the lines. (08)

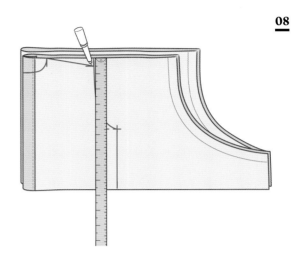

08

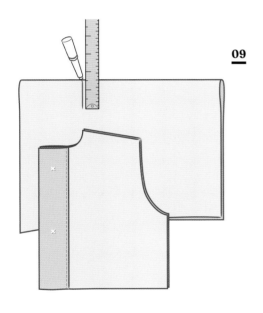

09

Peter Pan collar

These next stages can be done using contrasting fabric, if you like.

Measure the back neckline and subtract 1.2cm (½ in).

Unpick the side seam on one of the sleeves, open it out and fold it with right sides together. Place a front bodice piece on top as illustrated. Working from the fold, draw a vertical line the length of the back neckline minus 1.2cm (½ in). (09)

At the end of this line, place the front neckline minus the seam allowance, and trace the neckline to continue the line. (10)

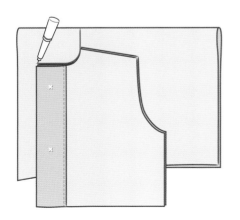

10

Measure and mark 5cm (2 in) from the curved line you have just drawn to make a larger curve below it; this is the outer edge of the collar.

Working from the front section of the original line, draw a curved line that meets the line below just before it curves. (11)

Use this shape as a template to cut out an identical piece of fabric and fusible interfacing.

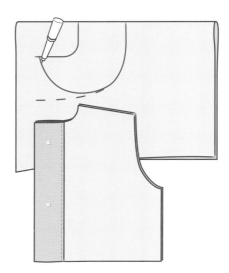

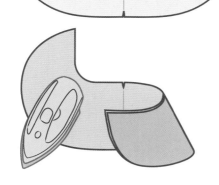

Using the iron, affix the interfacing to the wrong side of one of the pieces; this will be the undercollar. (12)

Cut this out, and notch the top and bottom of the fold with small snips.

Sleeves

To make the frilled cap sleeves, fold the other piece of cut-off fabric in half, with right sides together.

Place the tape measure at the top corner of the fold. Use it as a 'compass', pivoting to mark the first and second radius (see Pattern Pieces) from this point.

Cut out the shape, adding a 1.2-cm (½-in) seam allowance to the curved edges. (**13**)

13

Now taper the sleeve shape. From the middle of the open end, draw a shallow curve that connects to the lower curved edge (second radius) about halfway along. Cut this out to complete a sleeve.

Use this piece as a template to cut a piece for the second sleeve. Snip a notch at the top of the folds.

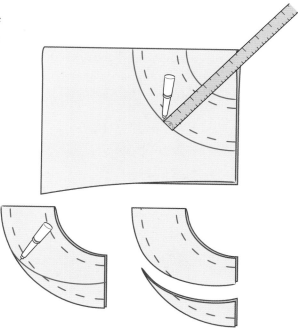

Prepare to sew

Now you're ready to sew. All the seam allowances for this project are 1.2cm (½ in).

14

Sew the collar

With right sides together, sew around the collar pieces, leaving the neck edge open. Clip the sewn seam and understitch the seam to the undercollar (the piece that was interfaced). Turn right side out. (**14**)

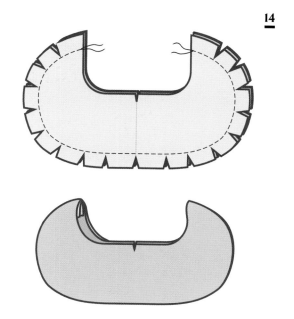

Bodice and collar

With right sides together, sew the bodice pieces at the shoulders and side seams.

Unbutton the bodice, and pin the collar to the neckline, with the right side of the collar facing the wrong side of the bodice.

Sew and clip the seams, especially where the angles are. Trim the seam. (15)

Turn the collar to the right side of the bodice. Press and topstitch this seam through all the layers, stitching 6mm (¼ in) from the seamline and enclosing the neckline seam. (16)

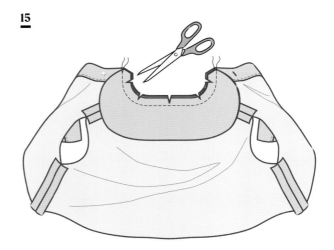

15

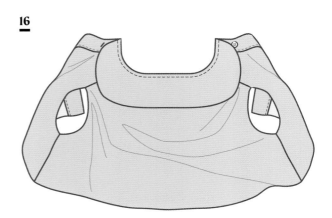

16

Skirt

Place the front and back skirt pieces with right sides together and sew the side seams of the skirt.

Sleeves

Fold the sleeve pieces in half, with the right side inside, and sew the edges opposite the fold.

Hems

This is optional, but I measured the hem's circumference and cut out a strip of the same length, 7.5-cm (3-in) wide, to extend the length of the dress and add a pop of colour.

Turn and sew a narrow double hem (see page 15) for the skirt and frilled cap sleeves.

Insert the sleeves

With right sides together, sew the sleeves into the armholes, matching the side seams and the notch to the shoulder seam.

Attach the skirt

With right sides together, join the skirt to the bodice at the waistline. You can either gather the fabric to fit or make box pleats.

Box pleat

Decide how many box pleats you want and mark their position along the waist seam of the bodice. Measure the bodice waist seam circumference and the skirt waist seam (this should be much bigger than the bodice waist). Deduct the bodice waist measurement from the skirt waist measurement and divide the result by the number of pleats you want. This will give you the width of fabric for each box pleat.

Versatile maxi dress

Maxi dresses are my go-to style when I don't know what to wear to an event. I think it's great to know how to make one, because it's a skill you can use over and over again The fit-and-flare maxi silhouette is a classic, with so much versatility that it never loses its relevance. You can use casual, smart, or dressy fabrics, and this style of dress can take you from lounge wear right up to bridalwear. Here I have gone for a casual look that includes some repurposed men's suit trousers: how's that for a transformation?!

Measurements (see pages 19–23)

Horizontal
Back
Bust
Underbust
Waist

Vertical
Shoulder to Bust
Shoulder to Underbust
Shoulder to Waist
Shoulder to Hem

Other
Apex

Pattern pieces for maxi dress
Skirt formulae:
(Waist plus 2.5 cm/ 1 in) divided by 3.14 and rounded up to the nearest whole or half number = first radius
(Shoulder to hem minus Shoulder to Waist) plus 4cm (1½ in) plus first radius = second radius
Skirt fabric:
(Second radius × 2) × second radius

Materials
Old suit trousers (preferably large-size men's suit trousers)
Fabric for overskirt: 4m (4½ yd) × 150cm (60 in) wide
Lining for overskirt (see page 157)
Lining for bodice
Bias binding: 2m (2¼ yd)
Zip: 56cm (22 in)

Equipment
Basic sewing project equipment

Method

Prepare the trousers

Fold the trousers in half and cut off the legs at the highest point by the crotch. Unpick the leg seams. (01)

With the right sides together, sew the front legs together along the inner leg seam using a 1.2-cm (½-in) seam allowance.

Repeat with the back legs, but sew with a tacking stich (this will be removed later when fitting the zip).

These sewn seams now form the centre front and centre back. Fold along the seams with right sides together and place the folded front piece on top of the back piece.

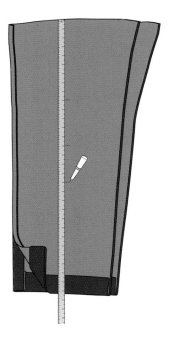

Place the vertical body measurements

Place the head of the tape measure at the top edge and measuring downwards, make three marks: at 23cm (9 in), Shoulder to Underbust plus 1.2cm (½ in), and Shoulder to Waist plus 2.5cm (1 in). Imagine these as lines running horizontally across the fabric: the first represents your bustline, the second the underbust line, and the last your waistline. (02)

Place the horizontal body measurements

Along the bustline, and measuring from the centre folds outwards, mark as follows with a small cross: (Bust divided by four) plus 5cm (2 in).

Repeat the formula for the Underbust and Waist, marking along the corresponding line with a cross.

Along the top edge (which will be the shoulder seam) measure and mark as follows: (Back divided by two) plus 1.2cm (½ in). (03)

Armhole

From the cross at the bustline, draw a straight 5-cm (2-in) line towards the centre folds.

From the mark at the shoulder, draw a curve for the armhole to the end of the 5-cm (2-in) line.

03

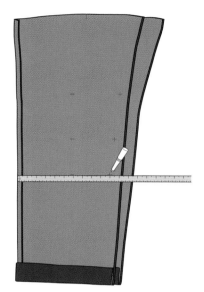

04

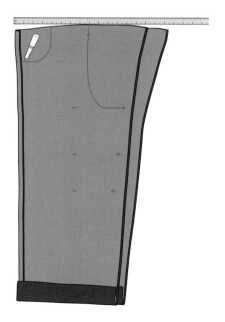

Neckline

From the top corner of the centre-front folds, measure and mark 10cm (4 in) downwards and also along the shoulder seam.

Draw a neckline curve that connects the two markings. (04)

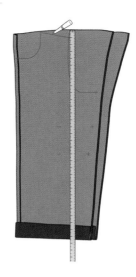

05

From the shoulder seam, measure and mark 2cm (¾ in) down the armhole. From that mark, draw a straight line to the top of the neckline. This slope is the shoulder seam. (05)

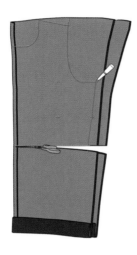

Bodice side seams

Join the crosses at the sides with a straight line to form the side seam.

Draw a horizontal line at the Waist.

Cut along the lines, then separate the front bodice from the back bodice and cut the front neckline lower (optional; do not cut lower than about 7.5cm/ 3 in). (06)

Princess bodice

Fold the front bodice and the back bodice down the centre with right sides together and lay on top of each other lining up the folds. Divide your Apex measurement by two and mark that measurement from the fold and about halfway down the bodice. Use the marks to fold vertical lines on either side of each piece, parallel to the centre fold.

At the waistline, measure 1.2cm (½ in) out from the fold and make a mark. Draw a vertical dart beginning at the apex and finishing at the waistline mark, then slant it outwards again below the waist.

07

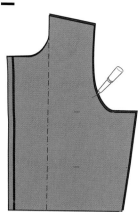

Working on the front piece, find the deepest part of the curve in the armhole and mark it. (Some sections of the armhole are more of a slightly bent line than a true curve; what you are looking for is the deepest part of the true curve.) (07)

08

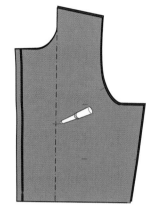

From the highest point of the shoulder seam, measure and mark your Shoulder to Bust measurement plus 1.2cm (½ in) along the dart crease. (08)

09

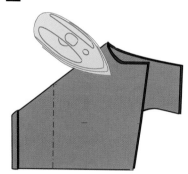

Fold and press what should be a diagonal crease connecting the marks made in the two steps above. (09) Open out the front piece. All the dart creases need to be towards the wrong side of the fabric, so fold and re-press as needed.

10

The armhole dart is 2.5cm (1 in) deep at the edge of the armhole (be aware that the edges may not match up when the dart is folded, but this is fine). Make a mark 2.5cm (1 in) from the crease, to the left of the crease line. Draw a 7.5-cm (3-in) slanting line down from this 2.5-cm (1-in) mark towards the vertical crease, but stopping 6 mm (¼ in) short of the crease. (10)

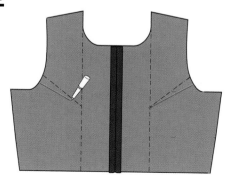

Prepare the skirt fabric

Cut a piece of fabric (see formulae in Pattern Pieces). Fold the skirt fabric in half crossways with the right sides together.

Cut out the skirt

Place the head of the tape at the top corner of the fold. Pivot the tape, using it as a 'compass', to measure down and mark the depth of the first radius with a series of regular marks. Repeat to mark the second radius.

Cut along the second-radius curve. Measure 1.2cm (½ in) above the first-radius curve and cut along this line, snipping a tiny notch at the top of the fold. This is the centre front. (11)

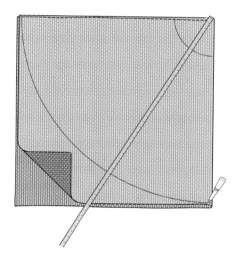

11

12

Sew the darts

Sew the bodice darts in one continuous seam, beginning at the armhole and adjusting the line as necessary. If you find that the front armhole has a step in the curve, or is very angular due to the dart, simply redraw the armhole curve, cut it out and reinforce the dart stitching. (12)

Sew the bodice side seams

With the right sides facing each other, lay the front bodice over the back bodice, making sure the centre front and centre back are matching, and the pieces are flattened out. You may notice that parts of the sides do not align, but that is fine. Pin at the Waist, Underbust, and then bustline.

From the centre front, measure and mark outwards along the bustline as follows: Bust divided by four.

Do the same with the Underbust and Waist, marking each along the corresponding line. (This will give you a very close-fitting garment; to add wearing ease, add 6mm (¼ in) to the divided number.) (13)

Join the marks with straight lines, and then copy the seam to the other side of the front bodice.

Sew the front bodice to the back bodice at the side seams.

13

Shoulder seams

Sew the shoulder seams with a 1.2-cm (½-in) seam.

Unpick the centre-back seam, test the fit of the bodice, and make any necessary adjustments in the side seams.

14

Lining

The fabric I have used for the skirt is transparent, so I'm lining it. To do this, cut a piece of lining fabric that is identical to the skirt. If you want a partial lining (as I have used here), make the second radius shorter than that of the actual skirt.

Hem the skirt lining. Place the lining over the skirt fabric, with the wrong side of the lining facing the wrong side of the skirt. Baste along the waistline seam and down the centre back, so that you are working with the two pieces as a single piece. (14)

Join the bodice and skirt

Pin the skirt waistline seam of the skirt plus lining to the bodice waistline seam, with the right side of the skirt facing the right side of the bodice, and with the centre-front notch on the skirt matching the centre-front bodice.

Sew with a 1.2-cm (½-in) seam.

Complete the skirt

Sew the centre-back seam of the skirt, with right sides together, from about 20cm (8 in) below the waistline. (You need to leave enough space to fit the zip, which will have the pull tab placed 6mm /¼ in below the neckline edge.)

Hem the skirt with a narrow, double-turned hem (see page 15).

Neck, armholes and zip

Follow the instructions for bias-binding the neckline and armholes (see page 15).

Insert the zip (see page 16).

One-shoulder jumpsuit

T rousers are a staple of any wardrobe, and the humble jumpsuit has held its place as a stylish classic. I was never able to wear one until I learnt to sew, as I could never find a store-bought jumpsuit that fitted me (many women find it difficult to buy trousers that fit perfectly; with an attached bodice, fitting issues may be increased). Hundreds of people have reached out to me about creating trousers, and I have waited until I was sure I could produce something where the fit would be perfect every time. So here is a stylish, one-shoulder, wide-legged jumpsuit, which will be flattering for most body shapes. If you're not ready to brave the single-shouldered look, simply keep both shoulders. You can add sleeves if you wish.

Measurements (see pages 19–23)

Vertical
Shoulder to Across Front
Shoulder to Across Back
Shoulder to Overbust
Shoulder to Bust
Shoulder to Underbust
Shoulder to Waist
Shoulder to Knee
Shoulder to hem

Horizontal
Back
Across Back
Across Front
Bust
Underbust
Waist
Hip

Other
Back Length
Back Waist to Seat
Inside Leg
Outside Leg
Thigh

Materials
Trouser-weight fabric: about 4m (4 yd) × 150cm (60 in) wide
Matching thread
Bias binding: 2m (2 yd) × 1.2cm (½ in) wide

Equipment
Basic sewing project equipment
Tailor's chalk in three different colours

Pattern pieces for one-shoulder jumpsuit
Bodice fabric:
Bust plus 38cm (15 in) × (Shoulder to Waist) plus 2.5cm (1 in)
Trouser fabric:
Hip plus 25.5cm (10 in) × (Waist to hem) plus 12.5cm (5 in)
Crotch depth formula:
Outside Leg minus Inside Leg

Back waist length (BWL) formula:
Back Waist to Seat minus crotch depth minus back waist length and mark this below your crotch depth line, draw a horizontal line across this point we will call this the back waist length (BWL)

Thigh length formula:
(Shoulder to Knee) minus (Shoulder to Waist)

Method

It is important to press all the folds you make.

01

Prepare the trouser fabric

Fold the trouser fabric in half crosswise (across the width; selvedges are at top and bottom) with the right side inside. Fold in half again along the width. The double folded edge is the outer leg seam, the top edge is the waistline area, and the bottom edge is the hem.

Draw a horizontal line 2.5cm (1 in) below the top edge to establish the waistline. (**01**)

Draft the horizontal measurements of the trousers

Near the top edge of the folded fabric and working from the outer leg seam, measure and mark as follows: (Thigh divided by two) plus 2.5cm (1 in).

Measuring from the waistline, in line with the half-thigh measurement just drawn, mark the depth of the crotch (see Pattern Pieces) minus 1.2cm (½ in). (**02**)

From the outer leg seam, about halfway down the line just drawn, measure and mark as follows: (Hip divided by four) plus 2.5cm (1 in). (**03**)

02

03

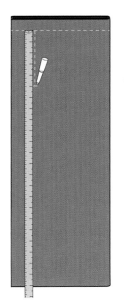

Draft the vertical measurements of the trousers

Work out the difference between your crotch depth and your back waist length and mark this below your crotch depth line. Draw a horizontal line across this point, which we will call the back waist length (BWL). (04)

Along the quarter-hip mark, draw a vertical line from the waist seam that is the length of the crotch-depth line.

From the bottom of this line, draw a straight line that extends beyond the crotch-depth line by 2.5cm (1 in). We will call this the crotch-base line (CBL).

Draw a curve in the corner of the 90° angle at the base of the quarter-hip line. (05)

Work out the difference between your Shoulder to Hip and your Shoulder to Waist. Mark this on the outer leg seam, from the waistline. This mark is your actual hipline (AHL). (06)

Inner leg

Along the waistline, from the quarter-hip line, mark as follows: (Waist divided by two) plus 5cm (2 in). From this mark, draw a curve to the AHL.

Extend the crotch base line to the hem. This is the inner leg seam.

From the end of the horizontal line below the quarter-hip line, draw a curve that smoothly joins the inner leg seam. (07)

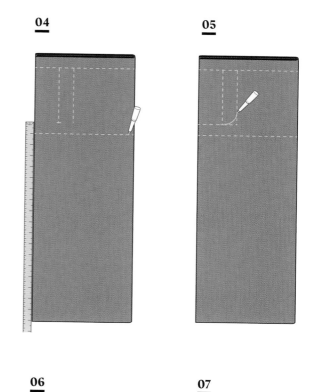

04

05

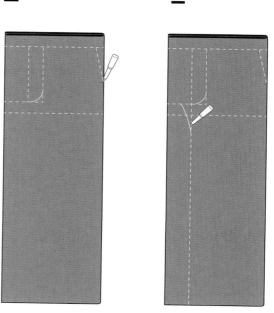

06

07

Front trouser and darts

From the quarter-hip line, along the waistline, measure and mark as follows: (Apex divided by two) plus 1.2cm (½ in), and then add 2.5cm (1 in).

At a depth of 20cm (8 in) below the waistline, measure and mark with a small cross as follows: (Apex divided by two) plus 2.5cm (1 in). This forms the point of the dart, and the 2.5-cm (1-in) space above is the depth of the dart.

Draw the dart. (08)

This forms the front trouser leg: mark the entire outer line and dart with one of the coloured chalks. (09)

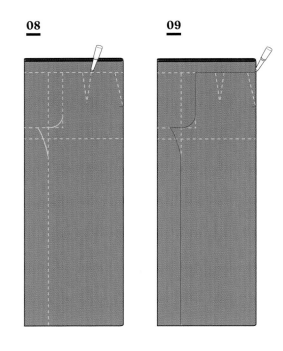

08

09

10

11

Back trouser

For the back leg, mark a cross that is 2cm (¾ in) beyond the CBL and 2cm (¾ in) below this line.

Draw a curve from that cross to the top of the curve at the front leg. (10)

Place a cross 1.2cm (½ in) above the waistline and 1.2cm (½ in) inside the front leg's centre-front seam.

Draw a diagonal line that meets the top of the curve you previously drew. This now forms the centre-back seam. (11)

From the cross at the base of the curve, draw a curve to meet the inner leg seam. (12)

Draw a diagonal line from the top of the centre-back seam to this point. This is now the back waistline.

Draw a curve from end of the diagonal line to the AHL. (13)

Back trouser darts

Working from the centre-back seam, measure and mark as follows: (Apex divided by two) plus 1.2cm (½ in), then add 2.5cm (1 in). The 2.5cm (1 in) is the width of the back darts.

Place a small cross inside the centre-back seam and 20cm (8 in) below the back waistline as follows: half-Apex plus 2.5cm (1 in). This is the point of the back darts.

Draw the darts. Use a different colour of chalk to draw out the back leg and dart. (14)

Complete the trouser draft

From the waistline, measure down to mark the knee length (see Pattern Pieces) and draw a horizontal line across the trouser leg.

Cut around the outer markings only, and through the outer leg seam folds. Notch through all layers at both ends of the knee line and the hipline. Carefully transfer the rest of the back leg to the third layer of fabric. The top two layers are the front leg. Don't forget to transfer the end points of the darts. For both pieces of the front and back leg, these points should be marked on the wrong side of the fabric for both legs.

12   **13**

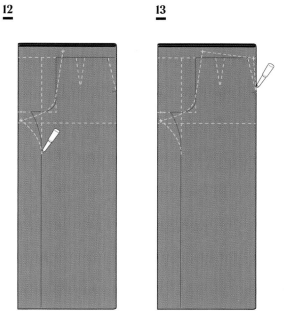

14

Prepare the bodice fabric

Work on the bodice fabric. Fold the fabric in half crossways (across the width, with selvedges at top and bottom) with the right side inside. The folded edge will form the centre front.

On both edges opposite the centre-front fold, fold over and press a 2.5-cm (1-in) zip allowance. Realign the open edges; this is the centre back. Bring the centre front over to line up with the centre back; these are the centre folds. The top edge is the shoulder seam and the bottom edge is the hem. **(15)**

15

16

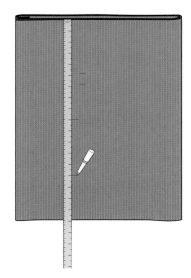

Place the vertical body measurements

Measuring down from the shoulder edge of the fabric, place a mark 23cm (9 in). This is the bustline.

Place all the other vertical measurements with an added 1.2cm (½ in), but omit the Shoulder to Bust and Shoulder to Waist. At these marks, visualise lines running horizontally across the fabric. **(16)**

Place the horizontal body measurements

Each of the marked vertical measurements has a corresponding horizontal measurement. Measuring out from the centre folds, mark along the Across Front line with a dot as follows: (Across Front divided by two) plus 2.5cm (1 in).

Repeat this for the Across Back measurement, but only add 1.2cm (½ in) rather than 2.5cm (1 in).

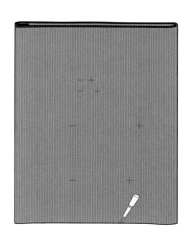

The Bust, Underbust and Waist measurements are divided by four, and then have 5cm (2 in) added. Each is marked along the relevant line with a small cross. (17)

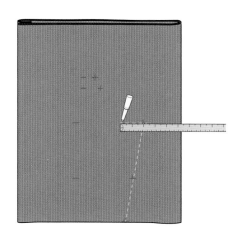

Side seams

Join the crosses from the bustline to the waistline with straight lines.

From the cross at the bustline, draw a 5-cm (2-in) straight line towards the centre folds. (18)

Neck

Measuring along the shoulder seam, working from the centre folds outwards, place two marks: at 9cm (3½ in), and at (Across Back divided by two).

Measuring down the centre folds from the shoulder seam, place a mark at 10cm (4 in). Draw a curve that connects this point to the first marking along the shoulder seam, this is your neck hole. (19)

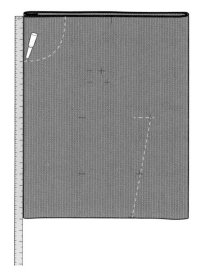

Armhole

From the half-Across-Back mark (the second mark along the shoulder seam), draw two armhole curves that land at the end of the 5-cm (2-in) line at the bustline. The first curve should intercept the Across Front cross and the second should intercept the Across Back curve. Both curves must be merged for the first 2.5cm (1 in) from the shoulder. **(20)**

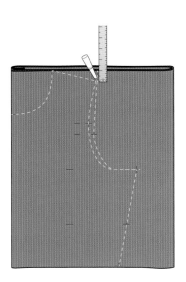

Shoulder

At the top of the armhole, measure down 2cm (¾ in) and draw a slanted line to the top of the neckline. This is the shoulder slope.

Cut out all the outer markings. Separate the front from the back and cut out the rest of the front armhole. **(21)**

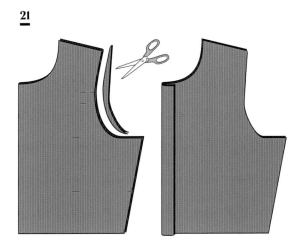

Make the bodice dart folds

Lay the front over the back again. Work out the Apex divided by two: create a fold down the length of the top at this point. Press. This is the dart crease.

Using an iron, invert all dart creases that project on the right side of the fabric to make them project on the wrong side of the fabric. **(22)**

The next few stages cover the darting of the bodice. Make sure that all darts are drawn to the left of the crease.

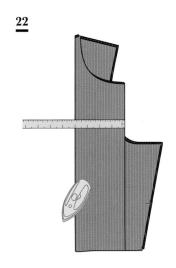

Back bodice dart

Work on the back piece of the bodice. The dart is 1.2cm (½ in) wide at Waist level, and tapers to a point 23cm (9 in) above the Underbust.

Establish the shoulder

Working on the front bodice, decide which shoulder you want to have as the single shoulder. Measuring from the highest point of this shoulder, mark your Shoulder to Bust along the dart crease. Also, find the deepest part of the curve in the armhole and mark just slightly above that.

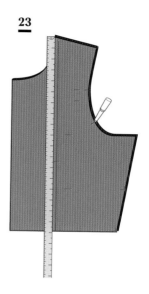

23

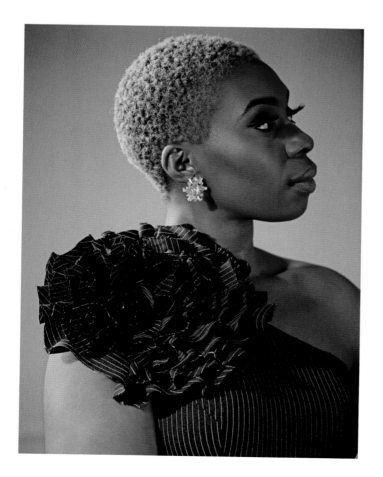

Unfold the front bodice piece. Working on the opposite shoulder, from the highest point of the shoulder seam, mark your Shoulder to Overbust measurement along the dart crease. (23)

Neckline

Draw a new neckline by connecting the base of the neckline at the single shoulder to the base of the armhole in the other side; use the Shoulder to Overbust measurement as a guide to how low the neckline should go. (**24**)

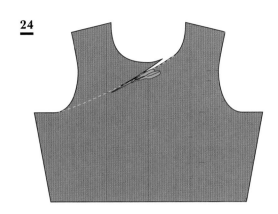

Lay the front bodice over the back bodice with right sides together.

Cut the new neckline through all the layers. (**25**)

Draw the front bodice darts

Working on the front bodice, the front darts are 1.2cm (½ in) deep at the Waist and Underbust level, then taper to a point 16.5cm (6½ in) above the waistline.

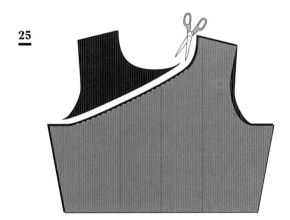

Bust darts

Work on the bust dart at the dropped shoulder. At the top of the dart crease, the dart is 2.5cm (1 in) wide. The dart tapers to a point 7.5cm (3 in) below this.

Working on the other shoulder, fold and press a crease between the two points you made earlier.

Marking on the left side of the crease, the dart is 2.5cm (1 in) wide at the armhole and then tapers to a point 7.5cm (3 in) along the crease and 6mm (¼ in) from the edge of the crease. (**26**)

Cut out the shoulder corsage

27

To create the shoulder detail, take two large squares of fabric, about 46cm (18 in) square, and lay one over the other with right sides together. Draw a circle with a 6.25-cm (2½-in) radius. Draw a cross inside the circle to establish a midpoint.

Within one of the quarters, draw a curve from the centre point to the edge. This will be the start of the spiral. (27)

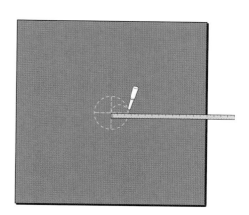

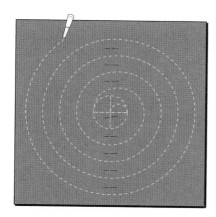

The lines of the spiral should be spaced out by 6.25 (2½ in) all around. Place some pins to hold the pieces together whilst you cut. Carefully cut along the spiral through all layers. (28)

Cut out two circles with a radius of 10cm (4 in), and matching interfacing pieces. (If you want a smaller corsage, feel free to reduce the radius – the finished product will be 2.5cm (2 in) bigger than the circle.) (29)

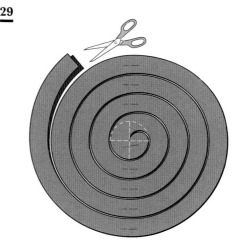

Sew the corsage

Affix the interfacing to the wrong side of both circles. With right sides together, sew the pieces around the edge with a 1.2-cm (½-in) seam, leaving a 5-cm (2-in) unsewn gap for turning the piece right-side out. Clip the seam. (30)

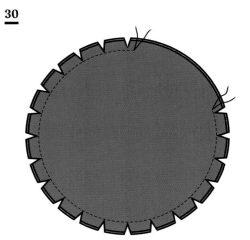

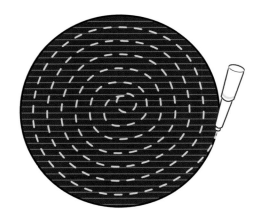

Turn the circle right-side out, tuck in the seam in the gap, and hand-sew to close the edge. This forms the base of the corsage.

Draw a spiral with 1.2-cm (½-in) spacing, as described above, from the edge to the centre of the circle. (31)

Sew the cut-out spiral strip to the circle, using the spiral you drew as a guide. Pleat randomly as you go: the more pleats you make, the fuller the corsage will be. When you reach the centre, cut off any excess spiral, leaving around 12.5cm (5 in) still hanging. Roll this 12.5-cm (5-in) remainder and carefully hand-sew it to the base.

Finish darts and seams

Sew and press all the darts in the bodice and trouser pieces.

Zigzag or overlock all the raw edges of the trouser pieces.

Completing the trouser section

Lay the front leg over the back leg, with right sides facing each other. Sew the outer leg seam with a 2.5-cm (1-in) seam. Make sure that the knee notches match: this is very important, otherwise the trouser legs will twist around the body when worn. Press the seam open. (32)

With right sides together, sew the centre back together. Repeat with the centre-front pieces. Press the seams open. (33)

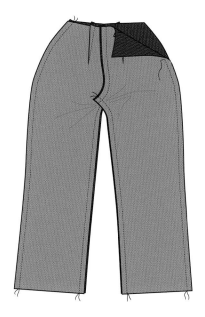

With right sides together, sew the inner leg seams. Unpick some of the outer leg seam on the side where the bodice has the dropped shoulder: only unpick about 25.5cm (10 in). Do not press out the crease that was formed when pressing this seam open. (34)

Test the fit of the trousers and make any adjustments.

Complete the bodice

Pin the centre-back seam of the bodice, with the right sides of the pieces together. Place the unfolded front bodice on top of the back bodice, right sides together. Match up the sides, pinning the pieces together 4cm (1½ in) inside the side edge.

From the centre crease of the front bodice, measure outwards along the bustline and mark as follows: Bust divided by four. Do the same with your Underbust and Waist. (35)

Join these marks with straight lines to establish the side seam, then copy to the other side. Use a long stitch length to sew the dropped shoulder side seam. Press the seams open.

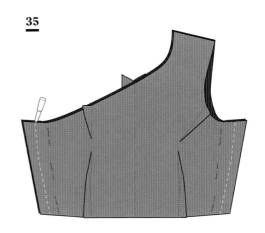

35

36

Sew the shoulder

Sew the shoulder seam of the single shoulder with a 1.2-cm (½-in) seam. Press open.

Test the fit of the bodice, and once you are happy, sew the centre-back seam shut and unpick the dropped shoulder side seam.

Neckline

On the front bodice piece, there will be a step at the top of the dart on the neckline, so redraw the line, smoothing out the step. Cut along the line. (36)

Join bodice and trousers

Match the bodice to the trousers at the waistline, making sure that the creases at the unpicked side seams are aligned. Sew with a 1.2-cm (½-in) seam and then finish the seam with a zigzag or overlock it.

Apply bias binding to finish the neckline and armhole (see page 14).

Zip

Sew the zip into the side seam, using the crease as a guide (see page 16).

Place the corsage at the desired spot on the shoulder, and carefully hand- or machine-sew it in place.

I'd like to thank God for the opportunities that my beloved gift have brought my way. I'd like to thank my amazing husband for his unwavering support and encouragement. And my beautiful daughter, whom this book is dedicated to – you are so so precious, I hope to make you proud.

This book wouldn't have been possible without that perseverance and dedication of the team at Pavilion. I am eternally grateful for the amazing opportunity and for buying into my vision once again. You guys are the best!

I want to thank all my family and friends, whose support and encouragement has pushed me on.